P H O T O G R A P H E R S ' B R I T A I N

GRAMPIAN

Jim Henderson AMPA.

FLOWER STAND, FRASERBURGH

PHOTOGRAPHERS' BRITAIN

GRAMPIAN

JIM HENDERSON

ALAN SUTTON

First published in the United Kingdom in 1993
Alan Sutton Publishing · Phoenix Mill · Far Thrupp · Stroud · Gloucestershire

First published in the United States of America in 1993
Alan Sutton Publishing Inc · 83 Washington Street · Dover NH 03820

British Library Cataloguing in Publication Data

Henderson, Jim
Photographers' Britain: Grampian
I. Title
779.94121

ISBN 0-7509-0119-5

Library of Congress Cataloging-in-Publication Data applied for

Cover photograph: Dunnottar Castle
Endpapers: *front*: Clachnaben; *back*: Hill of Corsegight
Title page photograph: Old Church, Forest of Birse

Typeset in 10/14 Sabon.
Typesetting and origination by
Alan Sutton Publishing Limited.
Printed in Great Britain by
The Bath Press, Avon.

INTRODUCTION

When my father gave me his camera some twenty-five years ago, I never imagined then that I would ever be publishing my photographs in a book. Sadly he will not know what he started as he died some five years later. I also have to thank him for another legacy – my birthright to Deeside. I have lived most of my life on Deeside, and my few years away from it both in England and overseas have only served to reinforce my love for this part of Scotland. I hope I have managed to project something of this in the photographs I have included in this book.

I couldn't have imagined at the outset of this project just how daunting a task it was to become. The photography aspect aside, I have found it extremely difficult to capture this large and varied region in only about seventy images. I make no apology for those areas or views not included, but challenge readers to search for themselves and to find all the wonderful aspects of Grampian that I have not managed to include. The publisher certainly set a challenging brief and I hope that you find I have met it.

Another aspect of the project has been the further exploration of the region. It has been a great pleasure to delve deeper into the hidden treasures of Grampian and I can honestly encourage others to do so. My sense of discovery of this region has been echoed by a discovery of new photographic standards. Acceptance that one's quality and attention to detail is not adequate is a very hard task: I hope that my skills are equal to this challenge, and that this book is testimony to the outcome.

The Grampian region has many different landscapes, from the mountainous Cairngorms, the picturesque glens and the rugged farmed hillscapes to the coastal plains of the Mearns and the fertile hinterland of the north along the Moray and Buchan coastlines. It is an area with innumerable historical artefacts, from the earliest habitations of man through the ages of Picts, Scots and up to modern times. The remains of burial cairns, stone circles, Roman camps, and ancient and more recent castles almost saturate the countryside. All these features have affected today's landscape in some way – old drove roads and river fords influencing the modern road system and the situation of towns, for example. The feudal land ownership pattern still influences much of the farming topography today. It is to the diligence and hard work of many farmers that we owe much of character in today's landscape, just as much as we do to the enlightened and committed owners of many of the estates that

BURN OF TILBOURIES, MARYCULTER

are covered with mature and sensitive woodlands, which we almost assume are part of our 'natural' heritage.

Modern Grampian cannot escape this ancient heritage and neither can the landscape photographer. Neither can he ignore the effects of the more recent evolution of the countryside, and particularly the effect of the population explosion and industrial development since the 1970s, especially relating to the oil industry. I have, however, made a conscious decision to exclude as much as possible of the modern, for example new housing estates, industrial sites and dual carriageway bypasses, as they are not the prime point of interest. But this aspect cannot be ignored, and is equally as important to the character of the region today as the views collected for this book.

As a landscape photographer both by inclination and profession, many of the changes do seem to be for the worse: out of character buildings, uniform housing estates, badly made mountain access tracks, electricity pylons and telegraph poles strung over lovely views, road widening schemes, commercial afforestation and so on. There is much left, though, that is full of character, and there does seem to be a genuine desire to conserve it where possible. The importance of tourism to the region has also made people more aware that the landscape and heritage of the region are its major attractions for the visitor. If that is not incentive enough to retain it, there will be little else to defend these qualities against the increasing pressure for change.

I have alluded to another debate that goes on in the region these days, and that is the dilemma between conservation and the pressures for expansion, modernization and leisure pursuits across a whole spectrum of activities. Many of these necessarily impinge on the environment directly and often to the detriment of the very thing that makes the activity attractive in the first place. It is not an insoluble problem, but the debate has to seek compromise, mutual understanding and the realistic acceptance of the true costs involved both in monetary and personal terms. Whatever the solution or the compromise someone will have to pay.

Finally I would like to thank all those friends and colleagues who have assisted me indirectly and directly with this project. I have had a great amount of support and much constructive advice. In the absence of a more formal acknowledgement, I am certain there are plenty who are glad I am not naming names; they are not forgotten.

St Cyrus Cliffs

St Cyrus is the first village one reaches on entering Grampian from the south along the signed coastal route. After leaving Montrose the traveller crosses the North Esk, passing a large sweeping railway viaduct on which the old and now disused link-line ran from Inverbervie to Montrose. St Cyrus is well worth a stop off and a short detour to the top of the cliffs by the village church rewards one not only with spectacular views but easy access to the lovely beaches below, with their cobweb of salmon nets disappearing into the surf.

I was a regular visitor to my two aunts at Pensioner Lodge, which had a link with a pensioned off soldier from the Battle of Waterloo, and there would await the familiar bucket and wooden spade for those pleasurable hours on the beach. The bonus, after the rather nervous climb down the sandy cliff paths, was not just the enormous flat sandy beaches, but the rocky end on one side full of rock pools teeming with small fish and crabs. These pools were lovely to paddle or swim in as they were crystal clear and warmed by the sun. There was a robbers' cave, The Kaim of Mathers – a nearby ruined castle on a peninsula, and the larger rock formations which had family names, such as the Lion Rock, the Leaning Tower of Pisa and the Chicken Rock. All had family stories linked to them by earlier generations.

Today the scene is still the same; busier of course, but now well protected as a National Nature Reserve. Its wealth of coastal fauna and flora is complemented at the southern end by a new visitors' centre and car-park. Set under the towering cliffs is the delightful little cemetery where there is Beatties' Grave, in memory of a local poet, George Beattie – who shot himself when the woman he loved married another. Quiet and lonely, with only the shriek of gulls and the wail of the wind to break the silence, the cemetery still evokes all the pain and sadness of this final desperate act.

HILL OF GARVOCK VIEWPOINT

Travelling north from St Cyrus along the coast road, the Bush Hotel is passed: memories of its association with one of the north-east's most notorious murders come to mind. Turning westwards at Lauriston to Laurencekirk the road winds its way upwards over the Hill of Garvock, and on the top we are offered this panoramic view over the Howe of the Mearns, from just above Laurencekirk, towards the distant Grampian mountains.

This basin to the south of the Grampians is referred to as the Mearns, and its name probably derives from its gift to Mernas, the brother of the ninth-century King Kenneth II. A rich fertile area of land, it runs southwards from Stonehaven through the Mearns villages of Drumlithie, Glenbervie, Auchenblae and Fettercairn before leaving the region. Laurencekirk is an ancient town, which was well known for its linen weaving trade and the Stiven wooden snuff boxes. Reflecting the richness of the surrounding farmland it is still an important market town, and as a child I always imagined it had one of the longest main streets in the world. Bypassed now by the main Aberdeen to Perth trunk road, Laurencekirk is not visited as much as in the past, but is certainly a splendid starting point for the trip across the Howe on the 'high' approach to the Grampians.

ROYAL BURGH OF INVERBERVIE

This rural scene shows the town of Inverbervie as well as its sheltered situation on the east coast. Travelling northwards along the coast road, past the small fishing villages of Johnshaven and Gourdon, the visitor arrives in this picturesque town on the south bank of The Bervie Water. A curving bridge with charming wrought-iron lamp standards along the top of the parapet walls straddles the north end of the river.

For four centuries Inverbervie has been a royal burgh. Hercules Linton, the designer of the famous tea clipper, the *Cutty Sark*, was born here in 1836, and the memorial to him is situated near the bridge. To the south, on the top of Bervie Brow, are the wireless masts of one of those 'secret' installations which always intrigued me as a youngster. Today my interest is more with the photographic opportunities of the nearby fishing harbour of Gourdon, with its daily landings of lobsters and crabs, and its picturesque harbourside studies of creel boxes and painted fishing boats, set against the largely unchanged village that hugs the hillside.

FASQUE HOUSE, FETTERCAIRN

Near the attractive village of Fettercairn under the foothills of the Grampians, and en route to the Cairn O'Mount, is a time capsule of Victorian and Edwardian life. Fasque House, dating from 1809, has been cleverly and authentically maintained to show how landowners and their servants lived at this time. Sir William Gladstone's home from 1829, the prime minister certainly enjoyed this connection with Scotland and in particular the shooting and fishing sporting life. The style of the house's exterior fascinates me as it is so very different from the Deeside and Donside properties, especially those of granite construction or related to the older baronial keeps.

One other attraction is the red deer herd which roams in the extensive parkland in front of the house, and which lies under the large oak trees on hot summer days. This is probably the closest most visitors will get to red deer in a trip throughout Grampian unless they are lucky enough to come across one of the Glen Muick herds, or see the odd one near the Linn of Dee. For most of the summer months deer stay well away in the high mountain passes, and are seen only rarely on the skyline. I always think Fasque and Fettercairn are ideal starting points for a 'Victorian Trail', as the house and the famous archway in the village both date from that period.

GLENBERVIE CHURCHYARD

One of the loveliest churchyards in Grampian for me is this one at Glenbervie and it is in part of the Mearns rich with Scottish literary connections. In the hut in the background are the restored tombstones of the forebears of Robert Burns. Burns's great-grandfather James Burnes, who is buried here, farmed on the slopes of the northern hills. The churchyard also contains many other old tombstones full of character and the history of the area, including the ancient remains of the Douglas aisle.

At nearby Arbuthnott there is a visitors' centre dedicated to the author Lewis Grassic Gibbon. He lived in the area, and it was one of his books, *Sunset Song*, that had such a notable success in a recent television adaptation. In the nearby Mearns village of Drumlithie is the almost Islamic structure of the weavers' steeple, a bell tower which in the 1800s controlled the working hours of the weavers in the village.

DUNNOTTAR CASTLE

I think this is one of the most spectacular settings for any of the Grampian castles. It certainly fulfils all my imagined characteristics of a coastal fortress and it is not too difficult to understand why it featured so prominently in a recent major film production of *Hamlet*. Although a ruin, Dunnottar is still intact enough to be dominating, perched on its rocky peninsula approached only by a steep path down the cliff face. It is situated south of Stonehaven, and nearby there is a panoramic view of the town, its harbour and the rugged coastline stretching to Muchalls and beyond.

Dunnottar Castle is an excellent example of the many castles throughout the region in terms of its historical perspective. It is a well cared-for ruin with some minor restoration, such as the Drawing Room, which gives some idea of the lives of the inhabitants in the past. The castle probably originated as a Pictish defensive site, and became ruinous after the 1715 Rebellion. Enough of the castle remains to convey the self-sufficiency of its defenders and also the brutalities of those far-off warring times. Particular points of interest include the Whigs' Vault, the cell where 122 men and 45 women Covenanters were imprisoned in 1685. The harshness of their treatment needs little imagination as one stands in that dark and dank dungeon.

Although this photograph was taken on a fairly benign day I would recommend that a visit to Dunnottar is made when there is lashing rain, strong and bitter winds, a thick sea mist shrouding the rocky outcrop and waves dashing themselves on the rocks below. Then the brutality that this ruin symbolizes, and the tales of drama and heroism, such as the saving of the Regalia of Scotland from Cromwell's forces in 1652, come alive.

STONEHAVEN

Stonehaven is in a sense the capital of Kincardine and Deeside, and although now bypassed by the main Aberdeen trunk road it has retained its busy quality. Situated in a dip in the coastline and with a sheltered harbour, one can see why our forebears chose to live in such a spot. The coast road climbing out of the town always seemed to me as a child like one of those twisting cliff roads in thriller films. Today the effect doesn't seem quite so frightening, but nonetheless the road affords spectacular views over the town and beyond.

The photograph is taken from the harbour which is always a popular place to spend an afternoon, eating in one of the waterside hostelries, receiving a gentle history education in the Tolbooth Museum or just enjoying the lazy luxury of watching others pottering around in small boats. Harbours are always exciting places for landlubbers like myself, evoking day-dreams of faraway places I will never visit – Robinson Crusoe memories from those dreary days at school in English lessons.

BOURTREEBUSH STONE CIRCLE, PORTLETHEN

As one travels north from Muchalls to Aberdeen along the coast, the much expanded communities of Newtonhill, Portlethen and Cove are passed. These have seen much of their character as small coastal hamlets swamped, as they have become commuter centres feeding Aberdeen. Housing estates, shopping precincts and industrial estates are all a reflection of the enormous expansion and prosperity brought to the area by the oil industry since the early days of exploration in the early 1960s.

Some three and a half thousand years ago equally major construction work was undertaken in the area. The results can still be seen in the remains of several 'Circles of the Moon': the main ones are those situated near Cairnwell – Hillhead of Aquhorthies and Bourtreebush, seen here. To the north, perched on a hill-top overlooking the new Portlethen golf course and the Badentoy Industrial Estate is the Craighead Stone Circle.

These circles are examples of the common Grampian form called recumbent stone circles: Craighead is an example of a 'Four-Poster', which probably had its antecedents in Aberdeenshire. The Aquhorthies (also spelt Auchquhorthies) circle is an excellent example of a later period construction, probably *c*. 1500 BC, and is one of the best preserved ring-cairn circles. In addition all these circles have vistas overlooking the coast and it doesn't need much imagination to see the attraction of such sites to those early settlers on the north-east coast of Scotland.

ABERDEEN HARBOUR

Aberdeen, now the oil capital of Europe, was once known as the Silver City because of the extensive use of the grey granite quarried locally. Once a major fishing harbour, its fleet is now virtually non-existent, and has been replaced largely with service vessels for the oil industry. This photograph illustrates the boats commonly seen in the harbour these days. The pilot boat waiting for its next call is berthed at Pocra Quay on a typical 'haar' day – when Aberdeen Airport can be shut down under a blanket of clammy sea fog, while a few miles inland there is scorching summer sunshine.

In the days of the large fishing fleets which would have filled the harbour to capacity, there would have been identifiable designs of boats for the different types of fishing activity. With the oil vessels a similar distinction can be made: those used as anchor-handling ships with their open rounded sterns are very different from those with squared-off high sterns used for carrying drilling stems or production pipes. There are also specialist vessels such as those for offshore survey or the very distinctive diving support ships with helicopter landing decks perched at their bows.

Another regular sight in Aberdeen harbour is the *St Clair*, the ferry that regularly commutes between Aberdeen and the Orkney and Shetland Islands. Among the usual flow of trading vessels from all over the world, occasional visitors include various naval units and the most celebrated annual event, the arrival of the royal yacht with members of the royal family on their way to Balmoral.

ABERDEEN: TOWN HOUSE AND UNION STREET

This is perhaps the centre of the City of Aberdeen, being the seat of the town council and the law courts. This Victorian façade was constructed in 1868–74, incorporating an old tollbooth dating back to 1615, although there were earlier tollbooths by the harbour quay dating from 1191. However, the first on this site was granted by Robert Bruce III in 1394 and so this whole area around the Town House and the Castlegate, the easternmost part of Union Street, carries much of the central history of Aberdeen. The little figure on Mannie's Well has moved around quite a lot, reaching this present spot in 1972. Mannie's Well is an old well house that probably started life in the early 1700s in the old fish market.

Lining Union Street, and most of the central streets of Aberdeen, are beautiful buildings that indicate the prosperity of the city during Victorian times. They are built of the local grey granite, which has given Aberdeen its characteristic style. Quarried from the now exhausted Rubislaw Quarry, now a huge hole about 130 metres deep, about 260 metres long and 130 metres wide, it supplied building material for houses as well as granite setts for roads until the late 1960s. Some of the streets are still paved with these hard-wearing cobble stones, although many were removed with the passing of Aberdeen's tramcars.

Aberdeen: King's College at Night

It was difficult choosing how to depict the character of the University of Aberdeen, and also the distinctive character of this area of the city – Old Aberdeen.

King's College is perhaps the best known of the buildings of the university, constructed when the institution was founded in 1494 by the then Bishop of Aberdeen, William Elphinstone. The chapel is noted for its Crown steeple, completed in 1506 and much admired as an impressive example of the late Scottish Gothic style. Opposite the college are the equally impressive Powis Gates, which with all the exotic flavour of miniature Arabian minarets add to the area's character. Nearby is the Channory and the cathedral kirk of St Machar, with its dominating twin-spired façade, built on the site of a kirk founded by the Irish St Machar around AD 580.

Not all that is of interest is that old, however, and in the Queen Mother's Library, in the new university complex, is housed the collection of some 40,000 original glass negatives taken by an Aberdeen photographer, George Washington Wilson. It is an extensive and invaluable record of Aberdeen and the north-east during the late 1880s. Obviously of general interest, it is a mecca for a photographer. My night study of King's perhaps has some historical value as well, being taken on the first night the college was floodlit in this total way.

Aberdeen from Banchory-Devenick

Hardly the heights but a view of Aberdeen that faces the traveller motoring into Aberdeen down the dual-carriageway from the south.

In the foreground is Leggart Avenue, one of the three roads heading westwards up Deeside. The very quick change from city into rural area is one of the delightful aspects of Aberdeen as a major conurbation and this view illustrates it well. In the distance can be made out the steeples and few skyscrapers in the city centre, and on the right the sea horizon is just discernible.

In the middle distance, right of centre, is the famous seven-arched Bridge of Dee dating from 1525. It is probable that some form of wooden structure existed from the late 1300s. Today this bridge is suffering from the inevitable pressures of traffic density, and several plans for solving the problem have run into equally inevitable conflicts between conservation and traffic flow. Perhaps the inevitable battle will be less bloody than the one fought in 1639, when the Covenanters led by Montrose forced their way over the bridge against the Royalist troops, and in which four Aberdonians were slain.

DRUM CASTLE, NEAR PETERCULTER

This castle is the first along Deeside after leaving Aberdeen. Set back from the main road, it is situated in a delightfully wooded area which is being cared for by the National Trust for Scotland's rangers service. The castle itself is beautifully maintained by the Trust and, like all its Grampian properties, the exploration of its interior is an exciting excursion into the history of a dominant landed family of the region. The recently reconstructed walled rose garden is part of the educational aspect of the Trust's work.

This photograph of the castle primarily shows the Great Tower, seven hundred years old, and the example which many other Grampian baronial tower houses followed. From 1323 the Forest of Drum was in the hands of the Irvine family, probably after being a royal residence from the time of King William the Lion. The Irvine family eventually gave up the property to the Trust in 1976. Several additions have been made to the castle over the centuries and its particular attraction for me is that mixture of styles. It was exciting to photograph a recent archaeological excavation of the inside of the Great Tower, in particular the unearthing of the old floor: one could imagine the huge cavern of a room with roaring fire, and the bustle of cooking and living going on side by side. There was even evidence that the rats had a healthy existence in their runs under the stone and wattle flooring.

VIEW FROM MEIKLE TAP, ECHT

This view is taken from the lower slopes of the Meikle Tap, at the eastern end of the Hill of Fare. It is an accessible walk through commercial forest on the Dunecht Estates, which cover most of the land seen in this photograph. Their policy of allowing natural regeneration above the developed forest is beginning to develop the whole Hill of Fare area in an attractive and sensitive way. Some of that young regeneration is visible in the foreground.

The estate has also maintained many of the original farm buildings, and the villages and various workers' dwellings have been well maintained in the style common throughout the estate. This policy, and that of maintaining the structure of the fields with their well-dressed stone dykes, has kept this part of the region attractive, as the view shows. Sadly perhaps the estate cannot contain the 'progress' of electricity pylons which are beginning to intrude unmercifully upon much of the countryside.

In the distance is the Loch of Skene, a popular boating area, which is shared happily with plenty of wildlife and supports a large flock of swans. In the background, just right of centre, is the large commuter town of Westhill, whose original population of around eight hundred when the oil industry began to develop has now increased to around six thousand. Beyond it is Aberdeen, and it is interesting that on a clear day it is possible to see the mass of Lochnagar about 80 kilometres beyond the Dee Bridge, but not the bridge itself, because of the topography of the Dee valley.

CRATHES CASTLE, NEAR BANCHORY

Further westwards from Drum Castle is Crathes Castle, the family seat of the local lairds, the Burnetts of Leys. Set against a small wooded hillside I find it surprising that the open area around the L-plan tower house and its particularly beautiful gardens are as spacious as they are. When viewed from across the River Dee which the castle overlooks, it always appears completely immersed in trees, and when the sun catches the walls, they seem to shine. This effect is from the distinctive use of harling – like pebble-dash but the covering is rather more like porridge and usually painted. This is a problem for any reconstruction work as the weathered harling is usually impossible to match. Harling is also a problem for photographers, as it gives an over-exposed area which modern camera meters cannot cope with, especially if the photographer is some distance away.

This view is taken from the gallery window and gives some idea of the setting of the castle as well as a bird's-eye view of its garden. Some of the original sixteenth-century yew trees which are a world renowned topiary feature may be seen, as can an avenue of trees planted recently, when the original avenue had to be removed because of disease. This castle, with its beautiful Scoto-Franco style, corbelling and turrets, and original painted ceilings in several rooms, is a fine example of how a family's fortunes turned on the strategic marriage to a daughter of the Church. As Keepers of the Forest of Drum the Burnetts had probably lived in far less comfortable quarters in a keep on the crannog in the Loch of Leys nearby, but their new-found wealth allowed them to build Crathes Castle in 1528. They took with them the famous Horn of Leys, reputedly given to the family by Robert the Bruce in 1323 for loyal service, and this still hangs in the great hall.

FALLS OF FEUGH

This is probably the most visited spot around Banchory, and rightly so. The beautiful tree-lined part of the River Feugh just above its confluence with the River Dee is a worthy setting for this plain three-arched single-lane road bridge constructed around 1790. Below the bridge are falls over large rock formations, now interfered with by man to make the path for the jumping salmon easier. It is that spectacle of nature that draws the crowds in their thousands: there is nothing more exciting to watch, or more difficult to photograph, than a salmon leaping into the frothing surge of water as it battles its way up to the spawning grounds in the Forest of Birse.

The photograph is taken from the viewpoint that most see the Falls from – a monstrosity of a steel footbridge, necessary because the single lane bridge couldn't safely accommodate both the traffic and the people. The other delightful aspect of this pleasant corner of Banchory is The Tollhouse, a quaint single-storey cottage, 200 years old and lovingly maintained by its owners. Set in an exuberantly colourful garden it is probably one of the most photographed private gardens in Grampian, and is an ideal subject for photographer and artist alike.

BANCHORY AND SCOLTY HILL

Set on the banks of the River Dee, Banchory is a town of some six thousand people which, like most of the Deeside towns, has seen considerable growth and expansion of the housing stock because of the influx of workers serving the oil industry. Although retaining much of its character, new houses to the north and the east have changed the town.

The most distinct feature that can be seen from Banchory is the tower on Scolty Hill (299 metres high) which overlooks the River Dee. Alongside the river is the golf course, which has given me many pleasant memories and even more of total frustration. Although the town has undergone many changes, some of them involving much local controversy, no other event has had more effect on its future development than the passage of the railway from Aberdeen in the 1850s. This was preceded by the construction of the first road bridge over the River Dee at its present site some fifty years before, both contributing to a development of the town to the west. Such changes are inevitable in any evolving community but this view is still much the same as I remember it from my schooldays.

This photograph hides much which is not photogenic – the new housing estates of box-like monotony and without any of the local building character of the past, the car-parks, boring shop-fronts, double yellow lines and traffic lights. It is, however, the character captured in this view that I want to record: the lovely wooded areas like my childhood haunts of the Captain's Wood and Bellswood which a recently formed Treewatch group is still working to keep intact. I make no excuse for using this view of my Banchory; I still think it is why the people love to visit the town and choose to live here. Only recently the tower has been restored, and occasioned Banchory's first royal visit, when HRH Prince Charles recognized the work of the local Rotarians in reopening the memorial to a forefather of the community.

ESSLIE THE LESSER AND FEUGHSIDE

This is probably my favourite place in the whole of Grampian, and on a lovely summer evening with a beautiful sunset I can think of no better place to go to enjoy not only the beautiful view but also to try to imagine the scene some three thousand years ago. Nearby there is the sister circle called Esslie the Greater, lower down and across to the left of this picture. A kilometre or so away and higher up to the east is the Garrol Wood or Nine Staines Stone Circle in the Forestry Commission's Garrol Wood plantation. Nearby trees have recently been cleared and its situation is much improved, although the distant horizon line is dominated by the Durris television mast. This takes away the sense of antiquity from that particular site.

The Esslie the Greater site was excavated in 1873 and some cremated bones were found, while the Lesser was excavated around the same time but nothing was found. Although the Lesser site is reckoned to be the worst preserved of the two it is its higher position and subsequent domination of the view towards Feughside and the distant hills that I find so exhilarating. It was from this spot that I enjoyed seeing Halley's Comet and its small but distinct tail during the last week of its appearance here.

These stone circles were probably some of the last to be constructed in Scotland and are therefore the youngest versions of some seventy-four recumbent stone circles in Grampian. There is evidence in a nearby forest of an early settlement which would have provided the manpower to construct this circle. Theories about the purpose of these constructions abound, but the simplest indicate that they were sites for religious ceremonies, cremation and burial, or early agricultural rituals. The Esslie circles are thought to be aligned by the position of the recumbent stone (like an altar) and its two flankers (upright stones at each edge of the altar stone) with the sunset in the case of the Lessler or the sunrise or moonset in the case of the Greater. Whatever, there is still an undeniable sense of agelessness when one stands by the circle and watches the dying colours of some rich sunset gently cloak the countryside in its nightly darkness.

FARQUHARSON COUNTRY

The countryside around Finzean and the Forest of Birse have become well known over recent years throughout the world, mainly owing to the paintings of Joseph Farquharson. Famed for his sheep and snow scenes, especially with a lovely orange sunset shining through birch trees, these paintings now adorn many a Christmas card, chocolate box and calendar. Although I live near the area Farquharson painted, capturing a similar scene on film is not nearly as easy, particularly as we hardly ever have the same depth of snow falling these days, and also because the sheep are not willing to pose. Farquharson, it can be supposed, had the same problem, because he copied model sheep when painting in his little caravan in the grounds of Finzean House.

This view looking over the Farquharsons' estate, is taken from the Strachan to Aboyne road just near Corsedarder, the supposed site of the burial cairn for the Pictish king Dardanas, who was slain at a spot now marked by a roadside marker stone. Across from this quiet evening rural scene is the Feugh Valley and on the right is the beginning of the very popular picnicking area of the Forest of Birse. It is also a lovely example of the characteristic birch and heather glen. From the Forest of Birse one can follow the source of the Feugh up into the hills to the Fungle, past the private shooting lodge of Birse Castle.

In the distance is Peter Hill (617 metres high), a steep walk but with interesting views across Feughside and with an attractive gorge on the far side. The Water of Aven, which joins the Feugh just to the east of Finzean near the Aboyne to Fettercairn road, at Whitestone, was an old halting place for the drovers travelling southwards after they had forded the River Dee at Kincardine O'Neil. A walker going up to the Water of Aven still has to ford the Feugh at the Mill of Clinter and still has to face the occasional winter spates or floods which can make the river uncrossable. This is an area with relics of a long history of occupation, as evidenced by burial cairns at Bucharn, Strachan or the Neolithic barrow on the skyline near this scene at Finzean.

RIVER DEE AT KINCARDINE O'NEIL

This particular view of the Dee shows off much of its character and the countryside through which it flows. The little village of Kincardine O'Neil has an ideal setting, nestling on the northern slopes of the valley, and has retained much of its original character. The maintenance of the traditional building style, untainted by the modern bungalow or English twentieth-century town house, has been partly luck and recently due to the wisdom of the local laird, who wishes to keep the village looking as 'traditional' as he can.

The village has a long history and the now ruined Old Kirk, dating back to AD 933, was founded by St Erchard. There is still a well bearing his name with spring water of high quality and supposed healing powers. The kirk is symbolic of the importance of the village as an important crossing point for the drovers heading southwards to the cattle markets in central Scotland. In the latter part of the last century the kirk itself was the setting for a thriving market-place, and it is possible that it was attached to a hospital erected by Alan the Durward in 1233.

The River Dee is one of the main salmon-fishing rivers in Scotland, and this stretch is frequented by fishermen from all over the world. The banks of the river from Kincardine O'Neil eastwards to the Potarch Bridge are an SSSI (Site of Special Scientific Interest), and even given the crowds of picnickers, swimmers and canoeists the banks are increasingly covered in wild flowers. The commercial forests around the area are also home to numerous buzzards which soar effortlessly in the thermals, and kestrels and sparrowhawks regularly hunt along the riverside fields. Herons share the river banks with the fishermen and what more lovely sight than to stand on the Potarch bridge and see the majestic heron tucked under the overhang of the riverside trees searching for fish.

AURORA BOREALIS, NEAR TORPHINS

This photograph of the aurora borealis is chosen from those I have recently taken at Crooktree, Kincardine O'Neil and is one of over seventy displays I have photographed since September 1989. This phenomenon is caused by the charged particles thrown out by sunspot activity exciting gas molecules in the earth's upper atmosphere. The quality of the display in terms of shape, extent to which colour is observed beyond the usual silvery white light, and the height above the observer depends upon its power, and thus the extent of its push southwards from the northern polar regions. Exceptional sunspot activity during the peak period of this current eleven year cycle has led to an extensive and prolonged series of displays, particularly as far south as Grampian.

The variety of the displays is difficult to describe, but their spectacular nature makes them one of the most exhilarating exhibitions of Nature to watch. To see a full corona, like a huge cathedral dome observed from the inside, but stretching upwards into the heavens while arms of colours – blue, reds, greens, pinks and yellows – moving upwards and around is one of the most awesome natural events. One half-corona I saw was like an enormous face floating among the stars: imagine what a Stone Age man would have made of it. Even the more ordinary displays, probably well to the north of Grampian, can be amazing. An arc, a very distinct curved band of pale light, may periodically surge and pale in intensity and then burst into great search-light beams stretching upwards, sometimes reaching almost overhead, and often moving sideways along the arc. Such a display may then die down for minutes or even hours and then begin all over again.

This particular photograph was taken looking slightly to the west of north (Torphins is just off to the right), and gives some idea of the banding or curtains of light that occur. Being in a rural situation means that there is little 'pollution' from street or house lights, a reason why the inhabitants of Aberdeen today are now unlikely to enjoy the lights that have made the song so famous.

ABOYNE FROM A GLIDER

The town of Aboyne is half-way along the River Dee, between Aberdeen and Braemar, and has grown very considerably as a dormitory base for many oil-industry personnel. It has also become a focal point for the surrounding communities because of its well-equipped Community Centre, with swimming and sports facilities as well as a theatre. Aboyne is perhaps best known for its annual Highland Games with traditional fairground attractions and a major regional pipe-band competition. Aboyne loch, once famed for the winter curling events or 'bon speils', is now recognized as one of the best water-skiing locales in Scotland, and is situated alongside that other Scottish sporting tradition, a good golf course.

This photograph gives an unusual view of this town and takes advantage of the gliding airstrip nearby. The glider is heading east, to where the valley begins to flatten out slightly. It is remarkable how from this height all the hills appear almost to be flat.

Aboyne has a long and important history, and from its various connections to early Scottish royalty it is the most important family seat east of Balmoral. Aboyne Castle, now private home of the Marquis of Huntly – 'the Cock of the North' – probably dates back to the eleventh century and is thought to have been a royal residence in the time of Alexander III. One of the Scottish castles handed over to Edward in 1291, it had a garrison of English soldiers at that time, indicating that even in those days Aboyne would have been used to the different sounds of foreign accents, so common on Deeside today. From 1388 both the castle and lands came into the possession of the present family, the Gordons, and it is the present Marquis who still presides over the annual Highland Games.

GLEN TANAR

This glen is becoming increasingly better known and visited, especially as this is encouraged by the young laird and his wife. I enjoy frequent visits to the glen on business and for pleasure, as it is an ideal starting point for several structured and educational walks, as well as being the beginning of the commonest route to the summit of Mount Keen (939 metres). In keeping with this educational theme it has a centre and ranger, and recently the estate has become a location for international orienteering competitions – which has meant that this area has found many new friends.

The photograph gives a flavour of the Tanar water, with its many picnic areas and a major camping site for guides and scouts from all over the region which manage to blend in quite unobtrusively. The bridge and tower at the entrance illustrate admirably the glen's extravagant past as a Victorian sporting centre. In the autumn the expanse of mixed woodland is awash with changing colour; a pleasure that can be indulged in as far as Balmoral.

LOCH KINORD

Loch Kinord and the nearby Loch Davan just west of Aboyne are well-known features of Deeside. Loch Kinord is passed by the main traffic flow and lies under the substantial hill of Morven ensuring that it is not easily missed. Loch Kinord is the only roadside loch along Deeside and lies in a picturesque setting among heather moorland and birch trees in the Muir of Dinnet Nature Reserve. This has been a popular picnicking area since Victorian times and the Cambus O' May Halt by the suspension footbridge over the River Dee was once a favourite stopping-off place on the old Deeside railway. Today the bridge and the nearby visitors' centre at the Burn O' Vat, with its viewpoint over the loch, are still very busy places on a summer weekend.

The loch side has plenty to offer, including the remains of habitation possibly from the Bronze Age. There is a fine example of a crannog (a man-made island created by sinking stones and tree trunks on to the loch floor): this is the island in the centre of this placid view from the north shore. On the far side of the loch is the main North Deeside road, through the Muir of Dinnet. Near to this point on the north side of the loch is the Kinord Cross, a fine example of late Pictish Christian carving. Towards the slopes of Culblean on the side of Morven, off to the right, is a rugged stone monument marking the scene of a bloody battle fought along the lochside in 1335, the Battle of Culblean. On the loch is an island which used to have a castle on it, although this no longer exists, that in its heyday possibly housed both Edward I and King James IV. Whatever its historical richness, the loch today is a place of peace and solitude, rich with wildlife, including the occasional osprey. It is one of the best places I know for passing a quiet afternoon, listening to the gentle lap of water on the shore or the breeze singing in the birches.

ARCADIA AT GRODDIE, LOGIE COLDSTONE

Still part of the Dinnet Estate, this delightful find came from an exploration up one of the many dead-end public roads in Grampian. I was delighted to come upon this ruined cottage set in a sizeable commercial forested area, with its immediate air of exotic eccentricity. A Grecian column on Deeside and a ruin that immediately felt like some ancient temple tucked away in the olive groves are little more than the sad reminders of some long forgotten inhabitant, which the weather, weeds and rabbits are gradually erasing still further.

From what I can find out from the memories of a few, South Milton Cottage was built in 1849 by one Duguid and was occupied up until the mid-1940s. The last occupant was known as 'The Painter', one Sandy Robb – who enjoyed indulging his fantasy imagination, moulding the columns and the circling band of leaves in cement, and filling the garden with statues and whatever else took his fancy. After his death, however, the cottage remained unoccupied and gradually fell into disrepair, probably assisted by damage in the great gales of 1953. The only reminders of the care and attention of the past occupants are the annual displays of snowdrops and daffodils when the spring snows clear from nearby Morven.

Queen's View, Tarland

This viewpoint on the Victorian Trail recently established by the local tourist board is best approached from the north along the Crossroads of Lumphanan road, because as one approaches the Slack of Tillylodge – a hollow in the hill – the great mass of Lochnagar suddenly looms up as the road drops away to the right. Here is the viewpoint with a Deeside Field Club marker showing all the hills, from Mortlich on the left to Morven on the right. Almost dead centre is the familiar outline of Lochnagar and in between a great spread of rural Deeside. Passing this point throughout the year one is afforded an ever-changing dramatic backdrop, as the clouds and sun are always vying with each other and the full sweep of the basin is an uninterrupted panorama.

Slightly further down the hill, towards Tarland, there is an example of some of the early occupancy of this area – the Culsh Earth House: a souterrain or storehouse. Of Pictish origin, dating probably from the early part of the first millennium AD, it was constructed by lining a trench with drystone walling and adding a roof of stone slabs. Covered with earth it gave dry and cool storage conditions for a nearby community, allowing them to retain a food supply over the winter months and thus remain in the area, rather than having a nomadic lifestyle. It is possible to crouch in the tunnel, which measures around 14 metres in length and is around 1.8 metres in height and width.

BALLATER AND LOCHNAGAR FROM TULLICH

Originally the most western terminus of the old Deeside railway, Ballater only came into existence on its present site in the late eighteenth century. This is a spa town, thanks to the properties of the waters at the nearby Wells of Pannanich, and was, as it is today, strongly connected with the royal family's visits to Deeside: it is only some ten minutes by car from Balmoral. Considered the 'capital' of the Deeside Highlands Ballater is well situated for good hillwalking on Craigendarroch, on the right of this photograph, and on the Pass of Ballater, to its right. On the left is Craig Coillach, which is a fairly steep and demanding walk but affords some excellent views to the west up the Dee Valley. In the centre is the towering bulk of Lochnagar which is a major rock-climbing challenge.

I have chosen this view because it illustrates well the basin in which Ballater was constructed. This view is the one that the motorist first has of Ballater, situated beneath the backdrop of Lochnagar; and from this small hill the road drops down on to the riverside flats. At Tullich, just behind this viewpoint, are the remains of Tullich Kirk. Probably the site of early Christian worship from Pictish times, it has some fine examples of Pictish carvings on view.

LOCH MUICK AND THE BROAD CAIRN

A few miles south of Ballater is the nature reserve of Glen Muick and the chance to see red deer. This very accessible loch has all the ruggedness of Loch Ness and the isolation of the best of the Cairngorms, qualities which have made it one of the most frequently visited places on Deeside. Inevitably there is a need to control the number of visitors, to arrest the eventual erosion and possible destruction of much that the visitor is attracted by in the first place. The royal family, who own the land, are attempting to cut back the number of visitors, possibly by restricting access to cars only – cutting out the ever increasing number of coach parties. The number of visitors all the year round has certainly restricted the royal family's use of the famous Royal Lodge of Glas-at-shiel at the top end of Loch Muick, because of the security implications.

Made famous by the publication of Prince Charles's children's story *The Old Man of Lochnagar*, and being the prime access route to this major climbing location, it does not seem feasible for any major cutback to be made, particularly as a public road runs to the rangers' park. In Scotland access to the mountains has been a long held 'right', and although this is understood to be dependent on the tolerance of landowners, the lack of a law of trespass means that it would be very difficult to prevent access to this beautiful countryside. Inevitably there are going to be clashes between the demands of the masses and the ability of the fragile ecosystem to cope.

This particular view of the Glen is from near the Black Burn, looking across to the Broad Cairn and the route to it by way of the Dubh Loch. The walk around the loch is very pleasant, and there are many opportunities to strike upwards for those wanting more of a challenge.

WINTRY LOCHNAGAR FROM MEIKLE PAP

This view of the summit of Lochnagar was taken from one of my favourite viewing points of the mountain, the smaller mountain top called the Meikle Pap. This is still a reasonable climb of 980 metres. This picture recalls my first real winter snow walk, when I spent most of the day sitting in a snow-hole on the saddle facing the corrie and lochan of Lochnagar. The conditions were awful, and in the almost perpetual white-outs the most I could see was the ice-axe standing about two metres away at my feet. I was perfectly safe and was quite content, after struggling through waist depth snow to sit the day out and see if there were any opportunities for photography. Eventually my patience was rewarded and a view opened up similar to the one in this picture. Unfortunately the photographs from that day are badly scratched and not of high enough quality to include in this book.

The current trend of milder winters has seen conditions change, with far less snow than there used to be, although Lochnagar remains one of the most demanding climbs in Scotland and part of the structure that attracts so many ice and rock climbers to it can be seen clearly across the lochan. In the summer months it is increasingly a popu-lar climb and is especially busy with hill walkers who seek, usually in vain, to see the midsummer sunrise. The views are also spectacular to the north and west where the main Cairngorm range can be seen quite clearly, beyond the two peaks of Cac Carn Mor (1,150 metres) and Cac Carn Beag (1,155 metres) which make up the summit of Lochnagar, and make it one of the highest peaks in the United Kingdom.

CAIRNWELL SKI CENTRE, GLENSHEE

Yes, sometimes there is enough snow for skiing on the mountains of Scotland. Certainly I recall that during my schooldays on Deeside we had so much snow that we were sick of it by Easter and desperate to get back to the golf again. Often we were sent home early from school and it seemed that places like Braemar were cut off for months. Today the problem seems to be that there is never enough snow for a hungry tourist and skiing industry.

The new restaurant in this picture on the slopes of Carn Aosda show the changes being made to cater for the enormous popularity of skiing. This particular centre on the main route from Braemar to Perth at the Cairnwell is building up a large summer industry as well, and the chairlift so necessary during the skiing season gives summer tourists the chance to scale the Scottish mountains the easy way. The views of the nearby mountains and Glenshee itself from the summit of Cairnwell (933 metres) are worth seeing. To fascinate the passer-by, some of the curious sculptures in the Glen Shee Sculpture Park are spread around on the nearby slopes. Similar to the Lecht, the road passing at these heights also gives the visitor a graphic idea of the clash between the conservation of the 'arctic' moorlands and the commercial developments of skiing, as well as indicating some of the pressures of large numbers of people on very delicate ecosystems.

GLEN EY

After a long pleasant walk along the flats of Glen Ey and following the course of the Ey Burn, peering into its tranquil peaty waters and seeing brown trout flit from stone to stone, the arrival at Altanour Lodge and the remains of a very old and small forestry plantation is the culmination of a truly enjoyable morning. It is then that one is thankful of the chance to dip aching feet into the cool waters, enjoy lunch and the good company of walking companions. My memories of this particular day are of scorching heat and the pleasure of paddling in that cool burn on smooth water-worn rocks. Not long after leaving this paradise we were drenched in a summer storm – unpredictability is part of the attraction of walking in Scotland!

Glen Ey is an attractive glen entered from a few miles west of Braemar at the hamlet of Inverey. Sadly it has been the scene of some recent controversy following the rather insensitive bulldozing of entry roads for access to the shooting moors. Retrospective planning constraints have forced a replanting programme, and given time most of the starkness of the roadsides should be removed. Given that most of the sensitively made access tracks do blend in well it is a pity when the occasional lack of thought for the beauty of the countryside occurs.

About 2 kilometres from the entrance to Glen Ey is a spot known as the Colonel's Bed. In this narrow rocky gorge on the Ey is the reputed hiding place of the Black Colonel, one John Farquharson of Inverey, after his escape from the Battle of Killiecrankie. This rocky ledge must have been very uncomfortable and not particularly well concealed from a diligent searcher.

GLEN OF DEE AND THE LAIRIG GHRU

Probably the best-known walk in the Cairngorms is the walk through Glen Dee past the source of the River Dee – the Pools of Dee – and through the Lairig Ghru pass to the Rothiemurchus Forest and eventually to Aviemore. This walk is very, very popular and is avoided by most solitary hillwalkers who want to enjoy the peace and solitude of the quiet, wide-open and untouched landscape of the Cairngorms. It is also, however, a part of the Cairngorms with a treacherous streak, and even on an August day it can kill. In winter the vicious nature of the arctic conditions in the Cairngorms has caught many an ill-equipped climber or walker unprepared for its ferocity.

This particular view was taken in August near the Devils Point, looking up into Glen Dee after the approach from Glen Derry and Glen Luibeg. Just discernible is the Corrour Bothy, many times a haven and lifesaver for those battling a freezing blizzard. The River Dee flows down from the distant pass between Cairn Toul and Braeriach on the left and Ben Macdui on the right. These are some of the main mountains for rock climbing in the Cairngorms, all three of them being over 1,000 metres in height. The area is a mecca for serious rock climbers from all over the world and is a popular winter training ground for many of the climbers eventually going on to tackle the world's highest peaks.

LOCH ETCHACHAN

This gives a clear idea of the kind of views that are found in the centre of the Cairngorms, and the typical moorland landscape. Taken from above the Coire Etchachan and looking away across the Beinn A'Bhuird Range on the left which peaks to some 1,196 metres, we can pick up the summit of Lochnagar under the clouds. The stream begins its journey down from Loch Etchachan under the rugged summit of Ben Macdui behind us into Glen Derry, and then eventually into the River Dee at the Linn.

Typical of the sort of day climbers often find, a cloudy start gave way to some sunshine. From the summit of Ben Macdui (1,309 metres) one could see as far as Ben Nevis on the west coast. However, as the clouds began to silently wrap themselves round the summits again like some deadly shroud it was wise to begin the steep descent as soon as possible. Soon this barren landscape was swept by squally rain showers, and by the time we reached the flatter area of Glen Derry, where the nature reserve plantations are fenced off to protect the recuperating Caledonian forest remnants from the onslaught of hungry red deer, the mountains were lost in a swathe of mist. But next week we were back again, trying another climb for a new and exhilarating view, just enjoying the fresh air, or taking in the majestic, empty, untouched and seemingly unending vista of mountains and sky.

THE LINN OF DEE

The Linn of Dee is a deep gorge to the west of Braemar beyond Mar Lodge, one of the most famous of the Victorian shooting lodges. The gorge is some 80 metres long and is as narrow as $1^1/_2$ metres in parts. Crossed by a granite bridge opened by Queen Victoria in 1857, the Linn is one of the most well-known sites on Deeside. Many peer into the rushing river hoping to see salmon leaping through the spray. During times of spate there is the pure fascination of seeing so dramatically the brute force of torrents of thrashing water forcing their way through such a small gap. Unfortunately some visitors have fallen into the gorge and have been drowned in the vicious undercurrents.

The photograph depicts the Linn and the bridge, giving some idea of the depth and ruggedness of the gorge. The best time to see it is in the dawn light as the sun rises, shining up the gorge and catching the bridge in its golden glow. This is the time when the red deer leave the nearby pine forests for the higher slopes and when the red squirrels are still collecting titbits from yesterday's visitors. And below the Linn as the sun climbs higher the river continues on its way, finding peace again as the gorge opens out and the clear water slips over wide deep brown pools under the majestic pine trees lining the river banks.

BRAEMAR FROM CREAG CHOINNICH

This is a view of the upper Dee valley which is probably not seen by many casual visitors to the area, even though it is only a short climb from the village of Braemar. The photograph gives a bird's-eye view of Braemar, the River Dee, and upper Deeside stretching beyond Mar Lodge and Inverey. To the right of centre is the Beinn A'Bhuird plateau. Ben Avon (1,171 metres), which is behind the outcrop on the right, is a distinctive mountain with its tors on the skyline – most dramatically seen by the motorist travelling past Invercauld House, just before reaching Braemar Castle. What a marvellous sight it can be when cloaked in late autumn snow, so dramatically setting off the wide meandering river and larches in full autumnal gold.

Braemar, probably the best known of the Deeside villages, is famous for its annual Highland Games, attended faithfully by the royal family since the days of Queen Victoria, as one of the highlights of their annual holiday at Balmoral Castle. The village is also a centre for hill-walking and skiing, as well as increasingly becoming the base for many of the coach tours which are commonplace in the area. Usually it also receives some notoriety as a low temperature centre for many of the winter weather reports, though perhaps not quite so regularly as it used to do – global warming perhaps?

Adjacent to the Clunie Water, a burn which splits the village in half, there is the ruin of Kyndrochet Castle, a hunting lodge for the eleventh-century Malcolm Canmore, with subsequent additions by Robert II and Kenneth II. Braemar Castle, which lies below the right outcrop and is a major attraction for visitors to the village, was constructed on the remains of an earlier castle in the 1750s. Farquharson of Invercauld, who had acquired the castle and estate, leased it to the government, and it was used as a barracks for General Wade's soldiers who were assigned the task of controlling the rebellious Highlanders. On this hillside, a little to the right (east) is the rock outcrop called the Lion's Face, but the trees that have clad the hillside for many decades have all but destroyed a semblance to the silhouette of a sitting lion. Nearby is the 'Charter Chest', a rock recess in which the Invercauld papers were hidden – as was the laird himself after the 1715 rebellion. On the valley floor the impressive Scottish Baronial style of Invercauld House can still be seen from the road as the traveller heads down the river into Royal Deeside proper.

OLD BRIG OF DEE, INVERCAULD

Spanning the River Dee between the estates of Invercauld to the north and Balmoral to the south, this is probably the best-known landmark on Deeside, and taken from the other side, from the new road bridge, the Old Bridge of Dee built in 1752 with its splendid central arch has probably appeared in more guises than there are chocolate boxes. Not that this is surprising, as its position over the River Dee with the backdrop of the White Mounth, part of the Lochnagar range, and the old Caledonian pines of the Ballochbuie Forest in the near distance catching the late summer afternoon sunlight makes this a scene not to be missed.

This particular view is a less common one, and made possible because of a low water level. This particularly exaggerates the central arch construction so common to the so-called General Wade bridges, which were narrow and hump-backed. Completed some four years after General Wade's death, and some fifteen years after he stopped constructing roads in the Highlands – he never constructed any roads in Grampian – this bridge was part of a programme of new military roads started around 1744. This is a good starting point for a very pleasant walk from Keiloch, passing behind the majestic Invercauld House in its lovely setting on the banks of the River Dee, and continuing into the heathery Gleann an t-Slugain. The Invercauld Estate has many lovely areas in which to spend a pleasant day walking.

BALMORAL CASTLE FROM CRAIG NORDIE

Not far from Balmoral Castle on Royal Deeside is a small birch-covered hill called Craig Nordie (488 metres) which gives some of the most breathtaking views of Deeside, including this one of the famous castle. The construction of the castle in this beautiful setting by Prince Albert in 1856, and the continuing connection with the royal families since the reign of Queen Victoria, have ensured its major role in tourism on Deeside. Without doubt it is this combination that brings thousands of visitors from all over the world to the north-east of Scotland, many of whom visit the Estate when it is open to the public each year. Many more continue to enjoy the connection with the Royal family's annual holiday to the area and in particular their Sunday worship at nearby Crathie church and their traditional attendance at the Braemar Gathering in September.

The castle was constructed of a light coloured local granite and the late afternoon sunshine makes this charming building come alive in its lovely setting of the Deeside valley. Across from Craig Nordie on the south side of the River Dee is the Balmoral Estate, stretching southwards to encompass the nature reserve of Glen Muick and the dominant mountain range of Lochnagar. From this vantage point several of the prominent cairns erected around the Estate by various members of the Victorian royal family can be seen.

Further to the west, towards Braemar, there are the remnants of the old Caledonian pine forest, much ravaged by the expanding red deer population, an expansion encouraged in the past couple of hundred years by the shooting on local estates as well as the removal of any natural predators, such as wolves. Unfortunately the general decline in the blood sports business and the high cost of culling the deer numbers is also exacerbating the situation. In the other direction from this viewpoint, beyond Balmoral Castle on the south Deeside road, is the Royal Lochnagar Distillery, and since its recent upgrading as a visitor attraction, it has become another heavily visited location, as have most of the distilleries within Grampian. The mix of farmland and forestry shown in the photograph is indicative of the nature of upper Deeside and gives it its scenic qualities that make it so popular with visitors. No doubt there will be a conflict when all these commercial forests have to be cut down, so that their economic potential can be realized.

GAIRNSIDE

A well-known route heading north from Deeside is through Gairnside, following the route of one of the old military roads past the garrison castle at Corgarff. Gairnside is a very characteristic Scottish glen: a single lane road with passing places and lined with birch trees, meanders through a pastoral landscape of small fields, with grazing sheep and the occasional croft. The road eventually arrives at Gairnsheil Lodge where there is a classic humpbacked bridge – flattened enough today to stop the buses getting trapped on the top like a seesaw.

This photograph celebrates something of the untouched character of Gairnside – difficult to capture, but a taste of the vibrance of the autumn colours comes across. This is Gairnside that goes nowhere: a delightful dead-end road is signposted Lary. The road threads its way up the eastern side of the River Gairn as it nears its confluence with the Dee, and captured here is the splash of golden birch and silvery aspen on a clear bright autumnal afternoon.

GLENBUCHAT CHURCH, STRATHDON

This very Scottish church hidden away in Strathdon's Glen symbolizes for me the hard life of these glens in their heyday, as well as the faith of their people. The church was constructed in 1473 following the tragic deaths of local people who were attempting to cross a swollen River Don to attend services at the then nearest church at Logie Kirk.

Even today a visit to this spartan building indicates that a service, probably lasting several hours, would have been accompanied by some discomfort – attendance would in itself have been a major test of faith. With the stone and earth floor and hard wooden pews, the interior hasn't changed for centuries. A favourite place of the Queen Mother and it is easy to understand why, with its simple charm and peaceful setting. Strathdon is a lovely glen along which to travel, and one eventually arrives at Bellabeg, the starting place for a journey up the Ladder Hills. This is a good walk through some characteristic sheep country and heather moorland.

Quite near to Glenbuchat church is Glenbuchat Castle, a well-kept shell of a former z-plan castle built in 1590. It is a graceful building standing high above the River Don, but is equally prominent from the approach within the glen. The corbelling and crow-steps set off what remains of the towers, but the many gun loops which still remain remind us of the troubled times in which these baronial homes were built.

KILDRUMMY CASTLE AND GARDENS

Dating from 1172, Kildrummy Castle is situated between two 'dens' or gorges. It was visited by Edward I, William Wallace and Robert the Bruce, and suffered several sieges, being periodically captured, destroyed and rebuilt. There are many stories attached to it from the payment of money to a traitor by pouring it down his throat in the form of liquid gold, or to the dubious manner in which the son of the Wolf of Badenoch married the very recently widowed Countess of Drummond in 1403. It is the sort of history that accumulates around most of these Grampian castles, and adds much flavour to the now sad ruins that stand among the clipped lawns and raked pathways.

Beneath the castle ramparts are the popular and much visited Kildrummy Castle Gardens, thoughtfully laid out among the rocky cliffs and around the bridge that is a copy of the original Telford Bridge over the River Don in Aberdeen. This replica was completed early in the 1900s by the then owner of the estate Colonel James Ogston, the original bridge being built in 1831. In 1954 the estate was sold to a Yorkshire businessman, James Pearson Smith, and today his widow continues to run the gardens and write local history books with equal enthusiasm and success. The new Kildrummy Castle was constructed across the Den in the 1900s by the Ogston family – known as 'Soapy' Ogston because of the soap manufacturing business they ran. This building is now a hotel beautifully maintained in its period splendour as are both of the other Ogston mansions in Aberdeen, Norwood Hall and Ardoe House – both hotels. The old Kildrummy Castle is maintained and kept in an excellent state of repair by the Historic Buildings Department,and not far away is the very picturesque Kirkton of Kildrummy churchyard, the gravestones perched around the top of a small hillock that sits proud in the sunlight, stark against the backdrop of Strathdon hills.

THE CABRACH

Travelling west from Donside towards Dufftown the traveller will pass through a large area of heather and peatbog moorland known as the Cabrach, named after a small hamlet of the same name situated on the A941. Taking the B9002 at Auchindoir on the Rhynie/Huntly road one really has a sense of the barrenness of the moorland on the slopes of The Buck Hill. As one joins the A941 and continues through the Cabrach, this sense of desolation is increased by the numerous ruins of farm buildings and crofts all along the route – symbols of the decline and changing nature of rural agriculture particularly in this part of the region. The Cabrach has always had a reputation for being an area that suffers from the onslaught of arctic winter conditions.

The photograph used to illustrate this area shows something of the desolation of this type of heather covered peatbog, and these dead trees symbolize some of the decay of the passing rural farming scene. This was taken in May on a walk to the summit of the Buck from which (particularly in the wintry conditions) there were depressing views all round of open moorland.

Not to be missed on the B9002 is the delightful late thirteenth-century church of St Mary with its extremely good example of Scottish medieval stonework, seen especially in the south doorway. The church is situated on a small mound above a tree-filled gorge, and on a quiet summer afternoon there is no pleasanter place to visit. The canopy of its majestic beech trees is so totally different to the treeless emptiness on the Cabrach proper.

TAP O' NOTH FROM THE CORREEN HILLS

Dramatic evening light is seen here from an ideal viewing place on the Bridge of Alford to Clatt Road, which crosses the Correen Hill range at the Suie Hill. The viewpoint, with excellent public display maps, looks over Knockespoch House to Rhynie which lies under the distinctive hill line of the Tap O' Noth. From this point we are looking north-westwards and Donside is below us to the south. On a clear day it is possible to see the Moray Firth.

The Tap O' Noth is a steep dumpy hill 563 metres high, on which there are the striking remains of a hill-fort dating from the first millennium BC. This is the second highest such hill-fort in Scotland and it is well worth the rather short but strenuous climb. There are some very worthwhile views as well – to the north over the vast forested area of the Clashindarroch Forest, past Huntly to the distant coastline, or eastwards in the direction of that other ruined hill-fort on the distinctive Mither Tap O' Bennachie. As the Tap O' Noth is rather like an upturned pudding in the centre of a basin the views all round are generally unhindered. One can certainly appreciate the attraction of the hill as site for a fort, with its clear all-round views and its steep sides, which would make it very difficult to attack.

HOWE OF ALFORD

Travelling downstream from Strathdon along the River Don we reach the Bridge of Alford, the crossing point of the river before the town of Alford. It is still a thriving market town that lies in a fertile valley under the Correen Hills and of course, as this view from Reekie shows, the distinctive hill-line of Bennachie. The Howe of Alford has a rich history and was the site of a battle in 1645 between Montrose and the Covenanters, memorable in that for once the Covenanters were beaten. There is also a stone circle, reminding us that the area was populated in prehistoric times.

Alford is a popular starting point for various trips around this area of Grampian, whether they are into Strathdon, Strathbogie or Garioch. It is itself a popular town as it has a large country park with a little railway and a transport museum. This is a lovely part of Donside and the river walks alongside the Don, especially at Haughton Park, give me much pleasure.

THE MAIDEN STONE, PITCAPLE

This single column of red granite is one of the few Class II Pictish monuments in the Grampian region and has relief carvings on both faces, as well as some on the edges. It is about 3 metres high and is in a prominent position at the side of the road. Situated in the parish of Garioch about 8 kilometres north-west of Inverurie, the stone is an excellent example of some of the later stages of Pictish carving. There are carvings of beasts and centaur, a two legged rectangle and Z-rod, elephant, mirror, and comb as this photograph clearly shows. On the other side appear a man between two fish monsters at the top (symbolizing Jonah and the whale), a cross, shafted and enriched and finally at the base a panel with enriched disc and Celtic interlacing.

Not only does this symbol stone show the early connection of Christian and pagan belief in the region but it is an example of the many relics of the past that exist in profusion on Donside. Some newer ones also exist, which although they may be more controversial, have their own charm. In particular I am thinking of the statue of Persephone, the Greek goddess of the underworld, whose return to the earth's surface heralds the advent of spring and the start of the new growing season. This statue was erected only a few hundred metres away from the Maiden Stone.

One legend has it that the Maiden Stone was named after the daughter of the Laird of Balquhain, a nearby stronghold, being on the site where she was mortally wounded after a scuffle following her elopement. Another much more colourful legend, recorded in Fenton Wyness's book, is that of Janet Maitland, a seventeen-year-old farmer's daughter, whose father's farm of Drumdurno was situated by the peat bogs on the northern slopes of the hill called Bennachie. While her family was away digging peat, the young lass was deceived into making a pact with a local warlock (witch): if the warlock made a safe path from the dangerous peaty bog to the house so that her family could return, then she would marry the handsome 'apparition' that confronted her. To her great consternation, when the path was formed the warlock returned to claim his reward – but Janet cried out that she would rather turn to stone than marry him in his hideous true form. In a blinding flash this is what happened: to many the elephant symbol is the warlock in disguise, and the mirror and comb are the sad symbols of the cheated girl.

BENNACHIE FROM NEAR KEMNAY

As one heads northwards from Dunecht, towards the town of Kemnay, there is a sharp corner in the road just before the entrance to Castle Fraser. At this corner there is a gate into a large field edged with trees and broom hedges – and the vista towards the hill range of Bennachie is a photographer's dream.

Bennachie and its distinctive knobbly summit at the eastern end of the range gives a very distinctive character to this part of Donside. This rocky outcrop called the 'Mither Tap' (518 metres) is now a mixture of granite scree and the still discernible remains of an early hill-top fort, probably of Pictish origin. Although a total ruin, some of the original walled ramparts can be seen, and it is still worth the fairly steep climb to see it, as are the uninterrupted views northwards to the Moray coast and eastwards to Aberdeen. It is obvious why this site played such a strategic role in those early conflicts with the Romans and other 'incomers'.

Not to be missed is Castle Fraser, another of the Grampian properties of the National Trust for Scotland. It is held to be one of the best examples of the Flemish style of architecture in Scotland. A magnificent round tower and a fifteenth-century square tower are combined in such a delightful way that from every viewpoint there is something new. The planned and landscaped woodland with some majestic mature pines and ash trees in which the castle is set make it a worthy example of the eighteenth-century improvement movement. The nearby town of Kemnay is an example of a thriving rural town with a mix of old and new, and is famed throughout the area for its fine pinkish granite used in many Grampian houses. Due to its very expensive extraction and dressing costs, however, this material is seldom used today.

INVERURIE AND THE RIVER DON

Sometimes the inconvenience of roadworks and a detour mean that one's usual route is upset. This was how I came to take this photograph, being forced to take the new bypass route around Inverurie. Looking from the new bridge over the River Don, the old road bridge is visible from a completely new aspect, also showing why there is such a lovely walk along the riverside, under the magnificent beech trees.

Beyond the bridge and slightly to the right, it is just possible to see the flat sponge pudding of the Bass of Inverurie. The Bass was the site of a Norman castle, which would have been the centre of this little community tucked in between the confluence of the River Urie and the River Don. In the cemetery that now surrounds the Bass there are some excellent examples of Pictish carved stones, and these along with other archaeological finds indicate that occupation of the area can be traced back to Neolithic times.

As it was situated at such a strategic point, the site's importance continued to grow throughout the centuries, from being established as the centre of the Earldom of Garioch in 1160 through to its continuing importance as a thriving town supporting both the agricultural, papermaking and oil industries. Inverurie is also on the main Inverness road and rail network and is at the crossroads for travel from the west of the region through to the coast. From Inverurie there is much to explore throughout the Gordon district and surrounding Donside, both from the ancient history of the area to the more recent, such as the remains of the canal that operated early in this century from Inverurie to Aberdeen.

HILL OF BARRA, OLDMELDRUM

The very early occupation of the area around Old Meldrum is indicated by the Kirton of Bourtie Stone Circle, part of which is seen here. Its recumbent stone is reckoned to weigh about 30 tonnes. Nearby, another excellent viewpoint at the Hill of Barra gives an even better understanding of the history and continuing prosperity of this large tract of fertile land running northwards and eastwards from the River Don. The hill itself is not particularly high (193 metres) but retains the distinct banks and ditches of a first millennium BC hill-fort, which is thought to have been in use until the Battle of Barra in 1307, at which Robert the Bruce won a small victory. This vantage point gives excellent views over Oldmeldrum to the eastern seaboard, also to Bennachie, and to the north-west to the Hill of Dunnideer, near Insch on which another hill-fort was situated. Beyond the Hill of Barra can be made out the Tap O' Noth already illustrated in this book, so overall one gains a picture of a thriving area where impending danger could be communicated by fire signals.

Across from Barra towards Bennachie is a hamlet called Durno, near which was situated a large Roman marching camp. It is possible that one of the largest battles between the Romans and the native inhabitants was the Battle of Mons Graupius in AD 83. Fought by Agricola, it was described too vaguely by Tacitus, the only author to record it, to give an accurate location, but one theory is that it was fought on the northern slopes of Bennachie. Incidentally this event might be the reason for Grampian gaining its name: an early translator of Tacitus, Francesco dal Pozzo incorrectly translated Graupius into Grampius.

Looking across this vista from the Hill of Barra today, the impression is of a patchwork of neat and fertile fields, a stream of traffic along the Inverurie road into Oldmeldrum, a hilltop town still retaining some delightful old houses bordering steep narrow closes.

HADDO HOUSE, NEAR TARVES

Haddo is one of my favourite National Trust of Scotland properties, mainly because it is not a castle! A beautiful and imposing country mansion, it has interiors which are dominated by paintings and elaborate plaster ceilings, and outside there are well manicured gardens. The flower borders at the back of the house complement the restrained and compact nature of this William Adam design, started in 1732 for the owner of the estate William Gordon, second Earl of Aberdeen. It is in marked contrast to the exuberance of another Adam design of the same time, that of Banff's Duff House. The borders also hint at the delightful landscaping of the surrounding countryside, which was complemented by the further work undertaken in the 1830s by the fourth earl, who enthusiastically planted over 14 million trees.

The front of the house is equally interesting, and although they are no longer used as the entrance the original curving stairs up to the first floor still exist. One can imagine the coaches arriving and elegant couples walking delicately up these stairs to some enchanted ball. This feeling is even more pronounced when the whole frontage is floodlit, as illustrated in this night-time photograph.

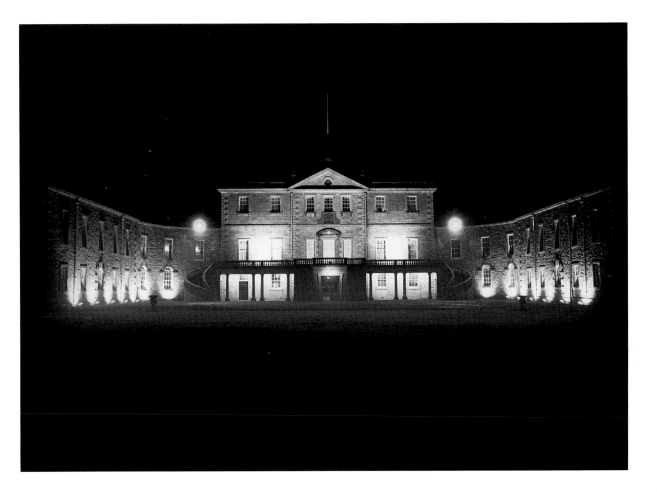

MILL OF TIFTY, FYVIE

The Mill of Tifty and Fyvie Castle are connected in the saddest of ways. It is a tragic story of love and death, and is captured in a lovely ballad by Andrew Lammie. Annie, the miller's daughter, fell in love with the castle's trumpeter, Andrew Lamb. Although the couple met and planned a future together, the jealousy of Annie's older brothers and sisters made them try to stop her seeing Andrew again. Annie suffered horrendous beatings as she resisted, and these continued despite Andrew's attempts to assist her. When the laird had to go to Edinburgh for a long period of time his trumpeter accompanied him, and with this loss of her love and his support Annie pined away. She succumbed eventually to the brutal beatings, which in the end broke her back after a fall. She died in January 1673 and was laid to rest in Fyvie churchyard where a tombstone can be seen to her, thanks to money raised by public subscription.

The nearby Fyvie Castle is not to be missed either, and is now carefully maintained by the National Trust for Scotland. At a cost to date of some £4 million this castle and its very valuable contents were purchased and completely restored for the nation. With this refurbishment now complete it is certainly worthy of a visit, particularly as in the present economic climate it might be one of the last collections of our early Scottish heritage to be so completely retained for the nation. Dating from the thirteenth century but with many major structural changes over the subsequent years, it is still one of the finest examples of the Scottish baronial architectural style. It offers the visitor probably the best staircase in Scotland, as well as some of the finest Scottish paintings by Raeburn. The last owner, who purchased the castle in 1889, was a Scotsman, Alexander Forbes-Leith, who made a fortune in the USA and gratifyingly continued to refurbish much of the castle. It illustrates perhaps the changing fortunes of these large properties today, where their continuing existence is very much in the hands of foreign tourism, and not in the hands of a few wealthy individuals. When they do pass from private hands, the only chance for their retention as insights into our past history lies with the wisdom and foresight of an understanding government.

ELLON ON THE YTHAN

Situated strategically on a natural ford on the River Ythan, the town of Ellon has always been a busy place, and now serves as one of the main commuter towns for the oil industry in Aberdeen, 17 miles to the south. The improved road network of recent years has much improved that journey since the 1970s when I first passed through the town on my way to the Peterhead oil service base that my employer was connected with. Today Ellon is bypassed by the heavy traffic, which makes it marginally quieter for the inhabitants and for the swans on the quiet flowing Ythan. It always reminds me more of an English river market town than those on the faster flowing rocky rivers of Dee or Spey, and banks of weeds beneath the old road bridge built in 1793 make that impression all the stronger.

Ellon's history goes back to around the year 400 BC when it was a major Pictish settlement, continuing to play an important role during the times of the Celtic Mormaers and the Normans. In 1308 the town was put to the torch by Robert the Bruce, but it has survived and was central in the gradual development of the agricultural success of the area up to the present day. There is a castle in Ellon of course, although the ruin is not open to the public. It is just visible in the wooded area in the background from this viewpoint. I still visit Ellon occasionally, enjoying the clash between the old town and the new, but even more the quick escape into pleasant wooded and fertile farming country – particularly where it follows the final few miles of the Ythan's meandering progress to the sea at Newburgh.

SANDS OF FORVIE AND THE YTHAN ESTUARY

Not living by the sea, I still have that childhood excitement when I get near it. I remember those very occasional trips we had to the coast on holiday when we were young, and all those memories of seaside boarding houses, shop fronts festooned with buckets, coloured windmills, beachballs and then the fun of sandcastle building and the feeble attempts at swimming in rather cold and rough seas. There was that salty smell in the air and something very refreshing in the experience of those alien seashore sounds and the sense of the never-ending movement of the waves. Some of those early holidays I spent around the East Anglian coast, especially at Great Yarmouth. It is to the Sands of Forvie that I go to relive those very early memories.

This estuary landscape is similar to the marshland around Yarmouth, for the Ythan meanders its last few paces before spilling into the windswept North Sea among the grass-topped sand dunes and wide expanses of empty beaches reaching all the way south to Balmedie Beach, north of the mouth of the River Don at Aberdeen.

The great desert-like dunes come alive as they are caught by the sweeping spotlight of the sun as it breaks through the stormy clouds, and the dull bronze browns turn into glistening whites like some beached Moby Dick. This old wreck, water worn, lies on the muddy foreshore of the estuary and is disturbed only by the fisherman as an ideal platform for their tackle boxes at low tide or by the odd gull having a snooze at high tide. Otherwise its peaceful grave is only disturbed by a few moored fishing smacks swinging in the tidal rip.

SLAINS CASTLE

Another of the popular visiting sites along the north-east coastline is Slains Castle, just to the north of the picturesque village of Cruden Bay at the mouth of the Water of Cruden – with its sandy beaches and golf course. It is very different to Dunnottar in all respects except that it is situated on the cliff face – so close, in fact, that one of its famous visitors in the castle's heyday remarked that it appeared to be a sheer continuation of the cliffs dropping straight into the swirling sea below. Although this photograph is taken on a day when perhaps there is pleasure to be found in just sitting watching the sea birds coasting along the rocky coastline to the nearby Bullers of Buchan, the real tale of this castle would benefit best from a dark stormy night of scudding clouds sailing across a witch's moon.

This is the castle famed for being the home of that very cuddly character of fiction called Dracula. Bram Stoker, Dracula's creator, stayed in Cruden Bay in 1895 and used the castle as the backdrop to his now infamous character. Even now, ruined as it is, it doesn't take a lot of imagination to understand why. Although dating back to 1597, Slains probably played its greatest role during the late nineteenth century as a popular place for the guests of the then Earl of Errol. Today the castle plays its role as a very impressive ruin, although it is in a dangerous state of repair. The cliffs along its frontage to the North Sea are also very dangerous if not treated with extreme care and have only recently claimed the life of a young boy. A further word of warning to the uninitiated: I do not recommend driving along the approach roads to the castle – only foolhardy and lazy photographers try that!

PETERHEAD HARBOUR

I have chosen to show a fishing harbour scene of Peterhead as this is what I have always enjoyed about the town, the largest apart from Aberdeen in Grampian. Although I originally got to know the town in the early days of the oil industry, it was at the fishing harbour that I would spend any leisure time. It was always a hive of activity and much more accessible than Aberdeen. Today it is the largest white fish port in Europe, and there is always a steady stream of refrigerated artics making their way to the south; along with the Fraserburgh lorries I still remember them from those annual holiday journeys along the A1 from Deeside to East Anglia.

Even with the enormous changes in the fishing industry and the cutbacks in fishing quotas, this port, along with Fraserburgh, continues to be busy. Once upon a time all these ports were packed out with herring fleets, reminiscent of those old photographs by the Aberdeen photographer George Washington Wilson, where the fishing boats crowded the harbour like sardines in a tin and were shrouded in a foggy haze of coal smoke. Today the crowded harbours are all but gone, although Peterhead is still the place to come for the early morning fish market to see something of the frantic nature of the industry when the fleet comes in. This photograph shows a Banff registered boat passing through the South Harbour on its way to the sea.

FRASERBURGH

Fraserburgh, like Peterhead, is another busy fishing port and is usually packed with boats from many of the other ports along the Moray coastline. Considerable expansion of both Fraserburgh and Peterhead is under way, and although Fraserburgh boasts some of the cleanest beaches in the area, the site from which this photograph was taken could do with some imaginative upgrading, particularly as it is one of the best-known aspects of the town. In the photograph is the Kinnaird Lighthouse, the oldest lighthouse in Scotland, built in 1787 on the remains of Kinnaird Castle (a tower house dating from the sixteenth century). The lantern house, converted from paraffin to electric in the 1930s, can be seen above another interesting building, the Wine Tower. This supposedly haunted chamber is all that remains of a sixteenth-century chapel which today is still accessible, but by appointment only. It has some fine examples of heraldic bosses that are well worth the trouble of getting inside.

Fraserburgh also has that air of a seaside holiday town, although in my experience there is a healthy, let's say bracing, sea breeze on the north-east coast. However on a boulevard along Harbour Road there are some pleasantly laid out gardens and a fascinating Victorian structure of over-detailed wrought-iron work, topped by a peacock. Strolling along the seafront, one gets a sense of the style of Victorian or Edwardian days. A walk along the boulevard in those times would have been a rarity, though, when making a living at sea or on the land would have been hard and all consuming.

GARDENSTOWN, MORAY

Along the Morayshire coastline are several delightful fishing villages tucked into little coves in the cliff face which have retained much of their individuality and the charm of their original architectural styles. Pennan has become perhaps the best known because of its location role in the British film *Local Hero*, but further along the coast towards Banff is Crovie and then Gardenstown, featured here. This particular view captures for me the real nature of these small harbours cosily carved out from the cliffs above. They have that real feel of a haven in a storm. A lot of new building has been allowed, particularly at Gardenstown, but none of it is visible from the harbour side.

Feelings probably run high at so much new building, and it is most visible from the little cliff-face churchyard of St John's church, whereas the nearby Crovie has been declared a conservation area and its original character has been largely retained. Gardenstown was a creation of the planned villages system, being founded in 1720 by Alexander Garden of Troup, and with the need for new houses throughout the region a popular place like Gardenstown will come under some pressure as a much sought-after location. The nearby churchyard of St John's precedes Gardenstown by several centuries, having been founded as a chapel in 1004 by the thane of Buchan in thanks for a victory over the Danes, the skulls of three of their chiefs having been on display in the church for some eight hundred years. The skulls have now gone, but the ruins of the church and the tombstones make a pleasing foreground for the vista of Gamrie Bay and the two villages hugging the distant sandstone cliffs.

THE ANCHOR OF MACDUFF

An excellent viewpoint from which to see both Macduff itself and the adjoining town of Banff is the high point on the cliffs at Church Road, where this old ship's anchor has been placed as a sort of unwritten memorial to the men who have braved the North Sea. Standing as it does in such a prominent position it is easily seen as one drives through the harbour front and past the tastefully maintained period buildings. Macduff, like many of the Moray fishing villages, was one of the new towns built around 1783 by the Earl of Fife, and is on the site of the village of Down. As the photograph shows these waterfront houses and shops overlook the harbour dockside, which is still a busy port with some fishing and associated shipbuilding activity. By strategically framing this photograph a large modern warehouse roof is surreptitiously hidden from view.

Standing on this high point there is a strong feeling for me of the harshness of the fisherman's life, and that tragedy when a boat sinks and the whole crew, often with several members of the same family, perishes in the force of some of the worst sea conditions imaginable. That ever present possibility has not diminished even with the advances of technology, and it has been reinforced in a different way for the region as the same extreme conditions often face the workers of the oil industry. It is perhaps difficult for a country-loon like myself to really appreciate that background fear, but when I see the simple cross that stands as a monument just behind the anchor then I am aware of that same sense of awe I had when as a youngster I saw the film *Moby Dick*, in which the harshness of the seafarers' lives was so vividly portrayed.

ROYAL BURGH OF BANFF

This photograph of George Street in Banff illustrates for me one of the charms of this lovely town, which is situated at the mouth of the River Deveron where it flows into the Moray Firth. It is full of a wealth of seventeenth- and eighteenth-century period houses, a great many of which have been preserved through the energies of the Banff Preservation Society which was formed in 1965. One has the ever present feeling that there is a strong community spirit underlying this movement, and this is echoed right along the Moray coastline in all the fishing villages and towns.

Banff itself is not a fossilized town, and whenever I have visited it always seems to be a hive of activity. It is a very popular holiday location with much for the visitor to see and do, as well as being an ideal base for exploring the many interesting places along the coast in either direction. Situated alongside a substantial golf course is the grand mansion of Duff House, now being restored. This extravagant building dates from 1725 and was designed by the architect William Adam for the brash MP William Braco. In total contrast to the contained elegance of Haddo House, this pretentious baroque-style house was never lived in by the owner after a bitter rift with Adam, and after an inglorious history came into the care of the State in 1956. I hope that once it is repaired it will have a happier existence as one of the many gems that Banff has to offer.

CULLEN

This view of Cullen gives some idea of the setting of the town on the seacoast of the Moray Firth, and shows its most well-known feature, the railway viaduct, which threads its way through the town. Opened in 1886 by the Great North of Scotland Railway, the viaduct added to the modern shape of the town, which was reconstructed from the 1820s under the patronage of the Earl of Seafield, the local landowner. As has already been indicated this was very much in the tradition of the region, and much effort during the great expansion of industry and population of the nineteenth century went into the construction and reconstruction of new or existing villages. Apart from the need to accommodate the requirements of the age, there was also the reflection of the aspirations of the local landowner in terms of the style and location of such projects, as was seen in the development of much of industrial England. This influence is seen particularly in some of the lovely buildings in the town square of Cullen. The viaduct itself came into being because of the restrictions placed on the railway's construction by Lady Seafield.

With a history going back 2,500 years to its existence as an Iron Age fortress, Cullen was made a royal burgh in the thirteenth century and King Robert the Bruce's Queen, Elizabeth de Burgh, died in the old village in 1327. The quaint area of Seatown retains its fishing village character and history of five hundred years in the industry, with smoked herrings and haddock giving the town its culinary claim to fame with a well-known soup called Cullen Skink. Renamed the village of 'Portlossie', Cullen also has a literary connection appearing in the writings of Scottish author George MacDonald. I suppose for most visitors it is the lovely sweep of Cullen Bay, the extensive sandy beaches and these magnificent remnants of the railway era, which sadly ceased to run along this line in 1967, that makes Cullen a popular visiting place on the journey along Grampian's north coastline.

BOW FIDDLE ROCK, PORTKNOCKIE

This is one of those natural eccentricities which never cease to amaze me. There is a baby version of this along the cliff face from Slains Castle, and both are remants of a historical past going back millions of years. The work of the sea on this incline of sedimentary rock has sculpted a unique formation whose name is easy to understand, at least for fiddlers. I wanted to show the cove and foreground as well, as it is typical of the coast along the north of Grampian. In these isolated and secluded coves a visitor can spend a quiet afternoon safely away from office traumas. Good cliff-top walks are another feature of this stretch of the coast and Portknockie is a good starting point for them.

Portknockie itself is a pleasant fishing village with a history going back to 1677, when the collective efforts of local fishermen set up the village, which is centred around its small secluded harbour among the rocky cliffs. The buildings in the village have been maintained to a very high standard in their period style. Painted in different colours but to match the various building materials and the way the blocks have been inlaid, they are a delightfully colourful spectacle. This is also a feature of the larger conurbation of Buckie further along the coast, where many of the early fishing cottages, where net drying lofts are still retained above the ground-floor living quarters. Nearer to Portknockie, the village of Findochty has also retained the style of house painting, and the bright oil paint colours give it a Mediterranean feel instead. The practice of painting in oil based material was to assist in keeping the winter weather at bay, especially the salt rain driven off the sea. This practice makes the area so different from much of Grampian, where the weatherproofing material usually used was plain painted harling – as shown in the photograph of Drum Castle.

Elgin is the largest town in the north-west corner of Grampian and as such is capital of the District of Moray. It certainly has plenty to offer both visitor and photographer alike, and some new vistas have been made possible with the opening up of parts of the town to accommodate the ring road system. This development has satisfactorily taken much of the traffic from the elegant town centre. Elgin has a long history, one of the most notable events being the establishment of its now ruined cathedral in 1224 on the banks of the River Lossie. It was sadly burnt to the ground in 1390 by the notorious 'Wolf of Badenoch', but rebuilt it continued to function until its lead roof was stripped away in 1567. The cathedral continued to decay until it was rescued from its role as an unofficial quarry for building material in 1825. Today some restoration and conservation is being undertaken, but the canopy of scaffolding and plastic sheeting would ruin photographs. It does, however, encourage the photographer to look beyond the obvious, and this photograph is the result of doing just that. It reminded me of those photographs one sees of Egyptian ruins and their statues with missing heads.

Much of the town's more recent history is still visible in Elgin, including some of the original eighteenth-century façades, narrow wynds and the old cobbled market-place. In the town centre is an island surrounded by roads on which the majestic Greek Revival-style church of St Giles stands. The ample seating and flower displays around it make an ideal resting place for the weary shopper. Overlooking the town on Lady's Hill is a tall column dating from 1839, with a statue of the last Duke of Gordon (1855). The hill is the site of a castle, of which there is now no trace, but which was occupied in 1296 by Edward I of England. The hill derived its name from the little Chapel of St Mary, and from it there are panoramic views.

CALIFER VIEWPOINT, RAFFORD

This viewpoint and picnic area near the village of Rafford, is a high point with an uninterrupted view over the Moray Firth, roughly above the town of Forres. This is an ideal spot to see the whole sweep of the coastline from the head of the Moray Firth at Fort George on the left right round to Burghead on the right. With binoculars the promontory of Burghead is plainly visible, and although little remains today it was probably the largest fort of any age in Scotland. It was Pictish in origin, but any ruins that might have been left were undoubtedly destroyed by the building of the present village in 1805.

The particularly unstable relationship between land and sea in this part of the Moray coast are illustrated by the distant Findhorn Bay, which has suffered over the centuries from the interplay between tide and river. Now a very popular yachting base this sheltered inland basin is ideal for amateur and professional alike. It is also an interesting point from which to see the aircraft taking off and landing at RAF Kinloss, which lies slightly to the left of centre. The other large aerodrome is that of Lossie-mouth, further round past the Burghead headland.

This is as far north as I have illustrated in this book, but given that there is still plenty more to see and do in the surrounding area, including a visit to the National Trust for Scotland's Castle Brodie, just a few minutes' drive from Forres.

Forres itself is famous for its many gardens and parks, and in particular its famous sunken garden and the annual floral displays which very often win regional and national Blossom Awards. This particular view shows one of the tree-lined parks at the north of the town. It gives me the opportunity to illustrate a feature common to every town, village and hamlet within the region – the war memorial in memory of those who served in both the World Wars. In some cases during the First World War all the young men from a small community were wiped out in one battle, and its effect on the region was often as devastating as has been the gradual attrition due to the changing methods of agriculture, or the early clearances of some of the larger estates.

Another relic in Forres of the region's past is worth a visit. The famous Sueno's Stone is the tallest and most comprehensively carved piece of cross-slab sculpture in Scotland. It stands some 6.5 metres high, and is a piece of fashioned sandstone slab weighing around 7.6 tonnes. Carved on all sides, it probably depicts a battle campaign against the Norse settlers of Orkney. This work by the local Picts is now covered in a plastic and metal shelter, making it almost impossible to photograph, but unlike many of the other artefacts which were carved from granite, the sandstone was very suscept-ible to damage by weather, acid rain and vandalism. Notwithstanding this cumber-some protection, the scale and detail of Sueno's Stone are still breathtaking.

PLUSCARDEN ABBEY, NEAR ELGIN

My memories of Pluscarden Abbey go back over thirty years, to when I was taken there as a young teenager by my English teacher and my aunt, who was *his* former English teacher. My memories of the serene Vale of Pluscarden and its abbey have remained with me ever since. The visit to photograph the abbey for this book was pleasing in that most of my memories have proved to be sound, and the beautiful building set in this forested and rural setting brought back that peacefulness I remember so clearly. Does the religious commitment give the place its air of serenity, or is it just the setting? This sense didn't last too long for as I was photographing this scene a military aircraft from nearby RAF Lossiemouth or Kinloss swept over the top of Heldon Hill just to remind me that I was in the twentieth-century.

The abbey, a fine example of a working abbey, was founded in 1230, one of three Valliscaulian priories in Scotland. It was founded by Alexander II and like most religious sites in Scotland had an unsettled progress over the centuries. In 1943, however, the partially restored priory was gifted to the Benedictine community of Prinknash in Gloucestershire, and in 1948 a committed restoration programme was begun. The abbey, as it became in 1974, today has an establishment of around thirty, and is widely recognized for its farming produce and stained-glass manufacture. Not far from Elgin, along the Miltonduff road, the visitor will have not only the pleasure of a drive through quiet rural countryside, but also views from the top of Heldon Hill, back to the lovely tree-clad Vale of Pluscarden. On the other side of the hill, to the north, are some excellent views of the Moray coastline – particularly now some commercial forest in Burgie Wood has been removed. Continuing along the hill line towards Forres, the Califer Viewpoint is reached: breathtaking views from there are illustrated earlier.

SPEYSIDE AT CRAIGELLACHIE

This view of the River Spey gives an idea of the gentler countryside which spans much of lower Speyside. Considerable commercial forestry is in evidence on all the surrounding hills, and the purity of the water from the many springs and burns means it is very active distillery country. As such it plays a major role within the region, situated not far from the so-called 'Granary of Grampian'.

Craigellachie is situated at the confluence of the River Fiddich and the Spey, and this Victorian village has not changed significantly over the years. A popular base for salmon anglers on the Spey, as well as being one of the starting-off points for walks along the Speyside Way, it is always a busy place. A pleasant walk up past Arndilly House through a tree-lined, climbing and winding road affords some lovely views of the Spey and eventually views of the distillery town of Rothes. From this town there is access to the nearby hill of Ben Aigan (471 metres) on which the Forestry Commission has recently initiated motorized treks to encourage more people to explore the forest and benefit from the views the hill can offer.

Craigellachie also has another symbol of the technological past on show, and this is a Telford single-span bridge which was prefabricated in Wales in 1814 and shipped up to Scotland to be constructed on site. A new road bridge means that the Telford bridge is now no longer used. Passing this point the Speyside Way takes energetic walkers on to the next stage, upstream at Charleston of Aberlour, where they can relax in one of the distillery centres dating from 1836 – not much younger than the town itself, which was a new town established in 1812.

BEN RINNES, DUFFTOWN

One of those disarming hill walks in which the height from the ground looks disconcerting, but as the ascent begins a series of plateaus take the sting out of the climb – that was my first experience of the straightforward climb up to the 840-metre summit of Ben Rinnes, just to the west of Dufftown. Apart from the views of this western edge of the Grampian region were the collection of tors, or scurrans – great towers of folded rock looking like some prehistoric outcrop of lava, and with all the mystery of the Easter Island heads. This view from the Scurran of Lochterlandoch to the south-east picks out the steepness of the hillside, and in the valley below is the glinting roof of the Chivas Regal distillery.

There are also some tremendous views to the north from Ben Rinnes over the River Spey to Roys Hill and Knockandhu Glen, with its famous distillery of the same name. Beyond there can be made out the distant forested area south of Forres around the Darnaway Forest, through which flows the River Findhorn.

This part of Grampian is the final frontier before we move into the hinterland of Speyside and into the Highland region. A mix of forest and mountain, it has a less well-occupied feel about it – but its clean mountain burns mean that everywhere there seem to be whisky distilleries.

FOCHABERS

The village of Fochabers stands on the River Spey and is perhaps one of the most visited locations in Grampian, thanks mainly to the existence of Baxters, world famous for canned and bottled Scottish food produce. Attracting some 200,000 visitors a year, catering for them has become a major facet of their business. Many of the visitors, of course, spend time in the attractive village itself.

This photograph is taken from a nearby viewpoint in one of the Forestry Commission plantations, and is part of a complex of woodland walks on the side of Whiteash Hill. This is perhaps the best general view and a walk to the cairn on the summit, although pleasant, does not afford particularly open views of the surrounding countryside, much of it covered in forestry plantations. This view of the village gives a clear idea of its essential layout, based along a single street. It was newly built in 1776 by the Duke of Gordon, because the original hamlet which was granted a burgh of barony in 1598 was too close to Gordon Castle.

As Fochabers is a conservation area, many of the original buildings have been protected, particularly in the High Street, and the character of the area is still as it was when originally constructed. I find the Victorian fountain in the centre of the village particularly interesting, as a structure of this kind on a similar scale is very rarely seen in the region. Alongside the new road between Elgin and Huntly on which Fochabers stands there is still, now a footway only, the last of several bridges that have spanned the Spey since 1804. This cast-iron bridge was built in 1854 and makes a very different foreground from the wide tree-lined Spey on its last stage before reaching Spey Bay and the Moray Firth.

KEITH

This photograph of the Strathisla Distillery shows why Keith is such a popular stopping-off point on the Whisky Trail or on the journey to Elgin. This distillery is one of the oldest in Scotland, established in 1786, and is still going strong. The manufacture of whisky and tweed were Keith's economic mainstays, although it has played numerous roles in the history of the region and Scotland for over 1,200 years. Much of today's Keith is a result of the town planning vogue of the eighteenth and nineteenth centuries: these were commonly part of the interests of the 'enlightened' landowners who saw possible business opportunities from the creation of new industries and the supporting infrastructure for the expanding workforce.

I also enjoy stopping off in Keith as it is the first of those towns to come – Elgin and Forres are the others – where they take their flower displays very seriously. Keith has a remarkable war memorial park and a bandstand park opposite a very elegant church. The splash of summer colours on the many flower borders at these various sites gives this long town some added attraction for the passing visitor.

HUNTLY CASTLE

Huntly Castle is probably one of the most splendid of the castles in Grampian, and even though a ruin there is enough left to show how magnificent it once was. Situated so close to the town centre, it must at one time have dominated the backdrop to the central area, although the avenue of trees softens that effect today. Built at the meeting of the River Deveron and the Bogie, the remains we see today are of the fifteenth-century palace and the subsequent additions by the powerful Gordon family, although there was a motte and bailey in existence as early as the late twelfth century. The sophisticated frieze at the top of the castle commemorates the first Marquess of Huntly and his wife, and dates from 1602.

Huntly itself is a thriving town, and although the main A96 to Inverness bypasses it, it is still very busy. This is probably because it is situated centrally in prosperous farming countryside, is a market town of consequence and has excellent fishing in the nearby rivers to attract the sporting fisherman. It is also close to distillery country. The commercial forests also become obvious as one passes Clashindarroch and the Bin forests, and this contributes as well to the prosperity of the town. However, it is still a town with much of its original character and apart from its very busy square there are many streets with pleasingly individual houses indicative of its past prosperity and confidence in the future.

LEITH HALL, NEAR INSCH

Easily reached from either Insch or the Strathdon to Huntly road, Leith Hall, belonging to the National Trust for Scotland, is a quiet and restful place. I always find it peaceful probably because of its pleasing compactness as a building, free from the imposing scale of the castles or the like of Haddo. Architecturally it has much to offer, because it has had many changes and additions since its inception in 1650. Being always kept in the same family – the Leiths (and Leith-Hays) – it has been well-documented, and the family heirlooms from past centuries have been lovingly kept. The whole feeling is one of continuity and evolution, and that sense seems to pervade the atmosphere.

There is a colourful and well laid-out walled garden which adds to the sense of timelessness, and one almost expects to bump into some aged gardener from times past still tending to the flower borders, although the sudden burst of a strimmer's shrill shriek soon shatters that daydream.

PICARDY STONE, INSCH

In a sense it is only right to end this book of photographs with a Pictish carving, as the Grampian region is so rich with remnants of this period from its past. I find the whole antiquity of the region fascinating and realize I have only scratched the surface in this book of what is to be seen.

Whatever we may think of these seemingly basic remains, whether scratches on a boulder or some tumbled down stone circle, one cannot help wondering at the effort and skill, as well as sense of community, that supported the movement and construction of such artefacts.

The Picardy Stone is apparently still in its original location, not discreetly tucked away in a churchyard. This handsome whinstone boulder was not dressed in any way, indicating perhaps that its origin was early in the evolution of Pictish carvings. Excavations have found evidence of a cairn and a possible grave site, showing a possible link between these symbols and the identification of a burial or memorial site. On this face pointing to the south are three clear and commonly found symbols, namely double disc and z-rod, serpent and z-rod, and a mirror – without the comb as on the Maiden Stone. This stands some 1.98 metres high alone in a field, and probably dates from the sixth or seventh century AD.

NOTES ON THE PHOTOGRAPHY

Any photographic work is demanding, and landscape photography has an additional problem, that of the interface with nature – its seasons, the weather, ever-changing light conditions, the wind, as well as the unpredictable human element – the off-loading of a coach tour of visitors at a historic site, the scaffolding that has appeared, or the delivery lorry that pulls up just as the sun comes out. The essential qualities for the landscape photographer, apart from any technical skills, are patience, a good eye for the weather and topography, a willingness to keep coming back and making luck happen for you. On rare occasions being able to spot the unique combination of elements which will make the 'great' photograph, and not messing up the technical side when it all happens – often within seconds.

Practically all the photographs in this book were taken during 1992, a reasonably average year in the Grampian region. The camera used was a Bronica ETRSi (645 format on 120 negative) and mainly with a 40mm wide angle lens. A yellow filter was used when relevant to maximize the contrast of clouds against blue sky. As a general principle I always stop down to f22/f11, thus operating at a relatively slow shutter speed – usually around $1/15$–$1/30$ of a second, and hence a tripod was a must. Focusing was on the foreground if relevant, but within the optimum depth of view arrangement for general distance sharpness. The wide angle gave a better combination of depth of field and, of course, a much wider sense of the landscape that was captured. Exposure times were taken from the camera's AE finder with bracketing for a zonal approach only used where very dark foreground and any essential detail was required. The film used was TMax (Kodak)100 *ASA*, processed in Acutol at a dilution of 1:20 for 14 mins (20 °C) with three hand inversions every minute. No development adjustments were made for exposure factors. Some older reproductions were from FP4 (Ilford) stock processed in either Aculux or Promicrol (now sadly departed) and these were usually developed with a continous agitator.

In the darkroom, burning-in was kept to a minimum and all the prints for this book have been done on Kodak RC paper – either Polycontrast III (the bulk) or Kodabrome II where a grade adjustment was required and developed in Ilford Multigrade Developer. The enlarger used was a now obsolete Lines and Jones 5x4 cold cathode tube light-source enlarger which gives almost grainless and very sharp prints.

TECHNICAL DATA

Key: B   = Bronica
N   = Nikon
Y   = Yashica
YF   = Yellow filter
RF   = Red filter
POL   = Polarizing filter

PAGE NO.	MAP NO.	TITLE	CAMERA	LENS	SPEED	STOP	FILTER
Front Endpaper		CLACHNABEN AND CAIRN O'MOUNT	B	40mm	1/15	f22	YF
Back Endpaper		HILL OF CORSEGIGHT	B	40mm	1/30	f22	
ii		FLOWER STAND, FRASERBURGH	B	40mm	1/15	f22	YF
iii		OLD CHURCH, FOREST OF BIRSE	B	40mm	1/8	f22	YF
iv		BURN OF TILBOURIES, MARYCULTER	B	40mm	4 secs	f22	POL
1	1	ST CYRUS CLIFFS	B	40mm	1/15	f22	YF
3	2	HILL OF GARVOCK VIEWPOINT	B	40mm	1/8	f22	YF
5	3	ROYAL BURGH OF INVERBERVIE	B	40mm	1/60	f8	YF
7	4	FASQUE HOUSE, FETTERCAIRN	B	75mm	1/60	f8	YF
9	5	GLENBERVIE CHURCHYARD	B	40mm	1/15	f22	YF
11	6	DUNNOTTAR CASTLE	B	40mm	1/60	f8	YF
13	7	STONEHAVEN HARBOUR	B	40mm	1/15	f22	YF
15	8	BOURTREEBUSH STONE CIRCLE, PORTLETHEN	B	40mm	1/8	f22	YF
17	9	ABERDEEN HARBOUR	B	40mm	1/15	f22	
19	10	ABERDEEN: TOWN HOUSE AND UNION STREET	B	40mm	1/60	f8	YF
21	11	ABERDEEN: KING'S COLLEGE AT NIGHT	B	40mm	8 secs	f11	
23	12	ABERDEEN FROM BANCHORY-DEVENICK	B	40mm	1/15	f22	YF
25	13	DRUM CASTLE, NEAR PETER-CULTER	B	40mm	1/30	f22	YF
27	14	VIEW FROM MEIKLE TAP, ECHT	B	75mm	1/15	f22	YF
29	15	CRATHES CASTLE, NEAR BANCHORY	B	40mm	1/30	f16	YF
31	16	FALLS OF FEUGH	B	40mm	1/125	f8	YF
33	17	BANCHORY AND SCOLTY HILL	B	40mm	1/60	f11	YF
35	18	ESSLIE THE LESSER AND FEUGHSIDE	B	40mm	1/15	f22	YF
37	19	FARQUHARSON COUNTRY	B	40mm	1/15	f22	YF

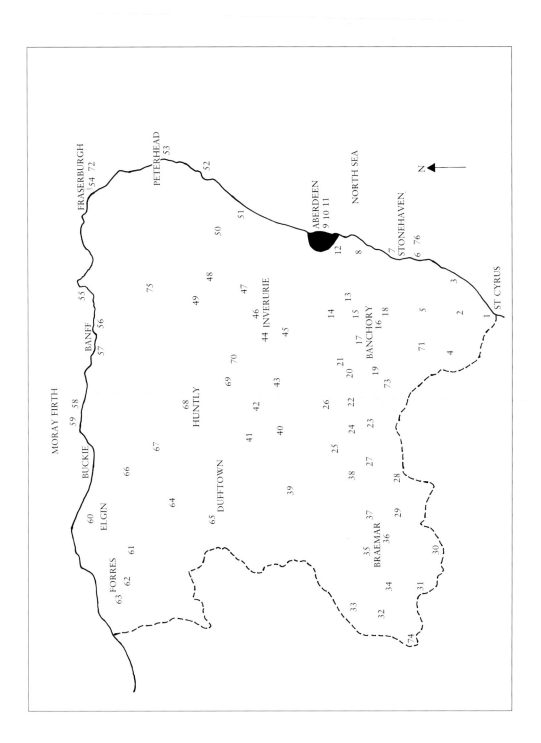

PAGE NO.	MAP NO.	TITLE	CAMERA LENS		SPEED	STOP	FILTER
39	20	RIVER DEE AT KINCARDINE O'NEIL	B	40mm	1/30	f11	YF
41	21	AURORA BOREALIS, NEAR TORPHINS	B	75mm	40 secs	f2.8	
43	22	ABOYNE FROM A GLIDER	N	28mm	1/125	f11	YF
45	23	GLEN TANAR	B	40mm	1/15	f22	YF
47	24	LOCH KINORD	B	40mm	1/8	f22	YF
49	25	ARCADIA AT GRODDIE, LOGIE COLDSTONE	B	40mm	1/8	f22	YF
51	26	QUEENS VIEW, TARLAND	B	40mm	1/8	f11	YF
53	27	BALLATER AND LOCHNAGAR FROM TULLICH	B	40mm	1/8	f22	YF
55	28	LOCH MUICK AND THE BROAD CAIRN	B	40mm	1/60	f11	YF
57	29	WINTRY LOCHNAGAR FROM MEIKLE PAP	B	40mm	1/30	f11	YF
59	30	CAIRNWELL SKI CENTRE, GLENSHEE	B	40mm	1/60	f8	YF
61	31	GLEN EY	B	40mm	1/60	f11	YF
63	32	GLEN OF DEE AND THE LAIRIG GHRU	B	40mm	1/30	f8	YF
65	33	LOCH ETCHACHAN	B	40mm	1/15	f11	YF
67	35	THE LINN OF DEE	B	40mm	1/60	f11	YF
69	35	BRAEMAR FROM CREAG CHOINNICH	B	40mm	1/60	f8	YF
71	36	OLD BRIG OF DEE, INVERCAULD	B	40mm	1/4	f22	YF/POL
73	37	BALMORAL CASTLE FROM CRAIG NORDIE	B	75mm	1/30	f22	YF
75	38	GAIRNSIDE	N	28mm	1/250	f11	YF
77	39	GLENBUCHAT CHURCH, STRATHDON	B	40mm	1/15	f22	YF
79	40	KILDRUMMY CASTLE AND GARDENS	B	40mm	1/15	f22	YF
81	41	THE CABRACH	B	40mm	1/60	f8	YF
83	42	TAP O'NOTH FROM THE COREEN HILLS	B	150mm	1/30	f22	YF
85	43	HOWE OF ALFORD	B	40mm	1/15	f22	YF
87	44	THE MAIDEN STONE, PITCAPLE	B	40mm	1/15	f22	YF
89	45	BENNACHIE FROM NEAR KEMNAY	B	40mm	1/15	f22	YF
91	46	INVERURIE AND THE RIVER DON	B	40mm	1/15	f22	YF
93	47	KIRKTON OF BOURTIE, OLDMELDRUM	B	40mm	1/60	f11	YF
95	48	HADDO HOUSE, NEAR TARVES	N	28mm	1 sec	f11	
97	49	MILL OF TIFTY, FYVIE	B	40mm	1/15	f22	
99	50	ELLON ON THE YTHAN	B	40mm	1/15	f22	
101	51	SANDS OF PORVIE AND THE YTHAN ESTUARY	B	40mm	1/15	f22	YF

PAGE NO.	MAP NO.	TITLE	CAMERA	LENS	SPEED	STOP	FILTER
103	52	SLAINS CASTLE	B	40mm	1/8	f11	RF
105	53	PETERHEAD HARBOUR	B	40mm	1/30	f11	YF
107	54	FRASERBURGH	B	40mm	1/125	f8	YF
109	55	GARDENSTOWN, MORAY	B	40mm	1/15	f22	YF
111	56	THE ANCHOR OF MACDUFF	B	40mm	1/15	f22	YF
113	57	ROYAL BURGH OF BANFF	B	40mm	1/15	f22	YF
115	58	CULLEN	B	40mm	1/30	f11	YF
117	59	BOW FIDDLE ROCK, PORTKNOCKIE	B	40mm	1/30	f26	YF
119	60	ROYAL BURGH OF ELGIN	N	28mm	1/250	f22	
121	61	CALIFER VIEWPOINT, RAFFORD	B	40mm	1/15	f22	YF
123	62	FORRES	B	40mm	1/15	f22	YF
125	63	PLUSCARDEN ABBEY, NEAR ELGIN	B	40mm	1/15	f22	YF
127	64	SPEYSIDE AT CRAIGELLACHIE	B	40mm	1/15	f22	YF
129	65	BEN RINNES, DUFFTOWN	B	40mm	1/30	f22	YF
131	66	FOCHABERS	B	40mm	1/15	f22	YF
133	67	KEITH	B	40mm	1/60	f8	YF
135	68	HUNTLY CASTLE	B	40mm	1/15	f22	YF
137	69	LEITH HALL, NEAR INSCH	B	40mm	1/15	f22	YF
139	70	PICARDY STONE, INSCH	Y	50mm	1/60	f11